Tales From A
Peak District Bookshop

by

Mike Smith

ALD Design & Print, Sheffield

Published and Printed by:
ALD Design & Print
279 Sharrow Vale Road
Sheffield S11 8ZF
Great Britain

Telephone 0114 268 6269

ISBN: 1 901587 01 0

First Published 1997

Dedication

To all my Customers

and

*To the memory of my mother,
who always made the most of life*

Contents

Preface

Shortly after my retirement from full-time teaching I was lucky enough to acquire a small piece of Paradise. My heavenly plot is a flat-roofed, one-roomed, oblong building, just twenty-four feet long, ten feet wide and eight feet high. When Jo-Ann and I first considered this little structure as a possible site for our second-hand bookshop venture, we were all too aware of its shortcomings - accommodation for no more than 4,000 display books, virtually no storage space, no separate staff room and not even a staff toilet. But both of us knew immediately that we would choose this tiny place in preference to all the other vacant shop sites which we had visited in the Peak District.

The possibilities jumped out at us: a corner site opposite Buxton`s busy Market Place; a curved, all glass Art Deco frontage which could easily pass as a Regency bow-window; a flat, white washed, black beamed ceiling which would give the interior a half-timbered appearance; and a small shop door with fifteen A4-sized panes of glass which would be ideal for the display of posters.

Once we had secured a lease on the premises, we knew that we would have to apply our minds in earnest to effective space utilisation and we realised that some lateral thinking would be required. The previous shopkeeper (a purveyor of electrical goods and late husband of Janet, our landlady) had served his customers from behind a vast mahogany desk placed near the back of the shop. We could not afford such luxury - the rear wall, like every other available area of wall space, would be required for shelving, and a large serving area would place unacceptable limits on customer circulation.

Just as we were about to dispense with the gargantuan desk, we realised that this splendid piece of furniture would make an ideal display table if placed longitudinally down the centre of the room. This arrangement would then leave just sufficient room for one set of island shelves alongside the old desk. After spotting a classified advertisement in *Loot*, I travelled to a private house in Mottram to buy a pair of identical seven feet by four feet bookcases which I found standing side-by-side along the wall of a living room. When Jo-Ann and I placed them back-to-back in the centre of the shop, we found that their collective width was exactly equal to that of our improvised display table, and their mahogany finish matched precisely that of the old serving desk. We decided that the gods must be good in our part of Paradise!

Our landlady kindly provided a wooden screen to mask the tiny sink and coffee-making area in the far corner of the shop; Bill, our next door neighbour, generously put to use his considerable carpentry skills to construct wall shelving; Jo-Ann contributed her painting skills to brighten the place up; former colleagues in the world of education donated books from their extensive libraries; I made many other purchases from private collections, sale- rooms and car boot sales to complete our opening stock; and David Huxley, proprietor of Buxton's Hall Bank Bookshop, generously gave me help and advice about the book trade. A carefully-worded advertisement, together with a photograph of the shop, was placed in the local paper and, by September 1995, we were ready to open our doors to the book-buying public.

Mike posing outside his newly opened shop.

I have been collecting books for half a century. All the contents of my personal library of some 2,000 volumes, whether they be paperback or hardback, old or new, scruffy or beautifully-bound, are precious to me and are certainly not for disposal. As I have never given away a book in my life, I made an early resolution that books from my own collection would not find their way into my shop, even if they happened to be on a customer's 'wants list'.

Given this book-hoarding habit of a lifetime, it was inevitable that I should find myself becoming attached to the books in my shop. Selling books is pleasurable because it is satisfying to see good books going to good homes, but also wrenching, because every sale is a book lost from the shelves.

Knowing that I must resist a strong temptation to hive off the most interesting books to my personal library, I decided to keep a notebook in which I could record the best passages and most telling pieces of information contained within the books in my shop. By this means, I hoped to salvage a few choice morsels from the feast of good literature which would pass through my hands. Then I realised that I had at my disposal another wonderful source of good stories and fascinating information. People who browse in second-hand bookshops provide a fund of tales, observations, witticisms and sound literary judgement. Within the first week of business I had begun to record their comments and conversations in my notebook too.

So began a series of notebooks which make up the contents of this book. I have never been sufficiently well organised to date my jottings or even to put my notebooks in order. As a result, there is no chronological sequencing of the notes in the following pages. I have simply unscrambled the jottings from my notebooks and arranged them in themes. The contents of this book are a reflection of the enormous pleasure which I have obtained from encounters with books and with customers during my first eighteen months as a Peak District bookseller.

Mike Smith
High Street Bookshop
June, 1997

Close Encounters of the Daily Kind

The corner shop was once the corner-stone of democracy - a forum where people could debate and discuss the issues of the day. The shop-keeper acted as a sort of news agency, gathering and disseminating the latest news and gossip. He or she also served as an unpaid social worker, providing a drop-in centre where lonely people could find much-needed company and have a friendly chat.

Out-of-town supermarkets have all but destroyed the corner shop, and most of the local stores which do remain have been converted into "mini-markets". The shop counter, formerly a place where conversation, as well as goods, was exchanged, is now a "check-out" where customers are processed as quickly as possible with the help of shopping trolleys, bar codes and conveyor belts

But shop based conversation is not completely dead; it survives in second hand bookshops. Bibliophiles

loiter with intent, and whilst they search the shelves for some previously-undiscovered literary treasure, they are all too willing to share their enthusiasms with the bookseller. Conversation often moves on from books to philosophy, politics and issues of the day.

Mary, a sprightly octogenarian, was muttering and cursing when she came in the shop today. When I asked her why she was feeling out-of-sorts, she said:

"It really is the last straw when people feel they have to help you across the road".

I had a moment of panic this morning when a customer declared:

"I'm having a baby. Can you help me?"

Just as I was considering whether High Street Bookshop could be turned into an emergency delivery room, my customer explained that she was looking for a book of babies' names to help her choose a name for her forthcoming offspring.

A group from Wigan came into the shop. They are in Buxton to support the pupils of St. Mary's School who will be performing at the Buxton Opera House tonight in the Gilbert and Sullivan Festival.

The members of the group described their local school to me in glowing terms, but I was surprised to find that their pride was based, not so much on the musical prowess of the pupils, but more especially on the headteacher's insistence that his students wear full school uniform!

A 75-year old man from Capetown asked if I could help trace the house in Buxton where his father was born. I rang Oliver, a reliable source of local knowledge, who found only one reference to the relevant surname in his *Buxton Directory* - a former landlady of the Swan Inn. My customer went off happily to the Swan in pursuit of his quest.

A young boy asked me for a book about dinosaurs. I found him a nicely illustrated large format book. "This is no good", he said. "I want one which contains photographs of dinosaurs".

Two retired headmistresses called in the shop. They told me that they were en route to the Lucian Freud exhibition in Ambleside.

When Jo-Ann and I paid a visit to a recent Freud retrospective at the Hayward, we were struck by the large number of female gallery-goers who had come to take pleasure in Freud's paintings of very fleshy ladies - female visitors to the show far outnumbered males!

I soon realised that my two ladies were fans of Freud for very different reasons. They took particular pleasure in two postcards of Lucian which they spotted on my pin-board: one is a photograph of a young and dashingly handsome Freud; the other is a self-portrait of a much older, but no less attractive Freud.

A couple who came into the shop this afternoon told me that they were staying in the Peak District village of Winster for two weeks. Their uncle, who is on holiday in the South of France, is paying them to stay at his cottage, in order that they might look after his dog.

This is the first time I have met anyone who has been paid to take a holiday in the Peak District.

A coach carrying a party of American tourists pulled up in the Market Place.

The shop was soon packed with brightly-dressed and brightly-chattering Americans, but their touring schedule was so tight that not one of them had the time to buy a book. Within five minutes they had taken their photographs of the shop's frontage and boarded the coach for Chatsworth.

I felt like an exhibit in a museum.

If it's Thursday, it must be Buxton!

A schoolboy came in and asked me if I had any books about the Devil. He wanted to find out more about the Devil for a project which he had been given for homework. A customer who was in the shop at the time suggested a novel by Denis Wheatley might be useful, but the schoolboy said he wanted "something factual".

Has there been another change in the National Curriculum?

A customer called in the shop this morning to purchase some Mills and Boon novels for her mother-in-law, whom she was about to visit. As my customer was in a hurry, she asked me to pick any three from the shelves. Hoping to provide a little variety, I deliberately chose novels by three different authors.

When I told my own mother-in-law about this transaction, she showed me an article from a *West Country Living* supplement in today's *Telegraph*. The piece was about Irene Swatridge, one-time occupant of Middlecombe Farmhouse and the author of no less than 250 books. During her prolific writing career, Ms. Swatridge used a variety of pseudonyms, including Virginia Storm, Theresa Charles, Irene Mossop, Lesley Lane and Jan Tempest. Most of her books were published as Mills and Boon titles.

So much for the variety pack of authors which I supplied to my customer this morning!

A customer bought a copy of Don McCullin's photo-journalism.

After flicking through McCullin's depictions of poverty, anguish and cruelty throughout the world, my customer said: "We hand over our lives to politicians in the mistaken belief that they will act as our representatives. We then find that they are intent on using us to further their own ambitions".

When my customer had left the shop, I took out my notes for tonight's Parish Council meeting and very carefully checked over the points which I had intended to make!

A lady sold me a boxful of books this morning. They included a *Teach Yourself Russian* pocket-book.

She told me that the Russian text book had been owned by a friend of hers who had gone through a marriage-of-convenience with a Russian musician who wished to leave the U.S.S.R. My customer's friend had conducted a contrived correspondence with the Russian lady and had learned enough Russian to give their "affair" some credibility. Eventually, the pair underwent a marriage ceremony (he has the photographs to prove it) and the bride was allowed to leave the Soviet Union. A quickie divorce followed. The Russian lady then settled in Amsterdam where she met a Dutch musician. Another marriage soon took place.

Mary came in today with her nephew who told me that he is the author of the current *Blue Guide to Greece*. He also told me that he had received no travel expenses whatsoever when undertaking research for the book.

I trust his guide contains useful hints on cheap travel!

I learned from one of my customers, who is a fan of David Hockney, that the Bradford-born artist's Californian house is the former home of Anthony Perkins, star of Hitchcock's *Psycho*.

It struck me that the artist and the actor have more in common than a shared house - they will both be remembered for their shower scenes!

Today is Valentine's Day.

A customer told me about her love life.

Once-upon-a-time she had fallen in love with her boss. Her boss told her that management-staff relationships were not allowed. He then arranged for her to attend a management course!

Jo-Ann has bought me Adrian George's *Paris in Autumn*, a day-by-day diary, in words and pictures, of one month in the City of Lovers (lovers of art, architecture, food, life, people).

Adrian George is a very talented artist. As a writer, he has a special gift for inventing collective nouns:

An inebriation of wines.

An erection of baguettes.

One of my customers told me she had just moved to the Peak District village of Elton from Ormskirk in Lancashire. Ormskirk has a quirky claim to fame - the steeple of its parish church is built alongside, rather than on top of, the church tower.

The linear village of Elton has some quirky juxtapositions too - the houses on one side of its street are built in gritstone; those on the other side are built in limestone.

I suggested to my customer that she might like to buy a book on follies!

A customer told me that he had been employed as a prison officer in Northern Ireland during the "dirty protest". He explained to me that the officers had faced considerable health risks during the protest, but that the prisoners themselves had not been at risk, as the possibility of catching disease from one's own excrement is very low.

Is this true?

A customer who came in the shop to buy books about the Yorkshire Dales told me that he's a member of a Pennine walking club. The club has no chairman, no treasurer and no constitution - its members simply turn up once a month at the car park in Horton-in-Ribblesdale and then set off for the hills.

My customer also told me that the club once came across Alfred Wainwright on one of his famous lone walks in the hills. But when I expressed my admiration for Wainwright's writing, my customer begged to differ; he suggested that Wainwright's knowledge of the land in which he walked was sadly lacking because, as a lone walker, he did not communicate sufficiently with other walkers and with local people.

Ronald Proctor came into the shop today. He showed me a cutting from the *Derbyshire Times* which reads as follows:

"Memories of V E Day celebrations of 50 years ago are still fresh in the mind of Ronald Proctor who lives at St. James Terrace, Buxton. Ronald writes:

I was wounded in Italy and, on coming back to England, I was taken to Chesterfield Royal Hospital. The Stavely Ward was given over to the military and I spent many months between there and Brambling House.

On V E Day those patients who lived locally and were fit enough went home. A few of us were left in the ward. After tea, a concert party arrived consisting of vocalists, a pianist and two girl dancers who did routines. The performance was very professional in every way and we had a wonderful time.

The concert party artists became our friends and visited us regularly and brought small gifts. I can only remember the name of one of the party. She was called Jean Barker. She helped to get me mobile. In her leisure time she took me into town and helped me meet people again".

Ronald then told me a heart-warming story:

Jean Barker renewed contact with Ronald after spotting his article in the local paper. She now drives over from Chesterfield to see him every week and takes him for car drives in the Peak District. "And do you know", said Ronald. "She can still perform the same dance routines and even do the splits!"

Ronald had to leave before I had chance to ask him how his fairytale was likely to end. He had to rush off and meet Jean!

Some Dutch tourists came into the shop today.

No matter where Jo-Ann and I travel in Europe we always find that Dutch tourists are much in evidence. The Netherlands must empty of people in the summer, save for the tourists who come to admire a country from which the inhabitants are so keen to escape!

The wife of a customer who buys books from me on photography told me that she is often asked to act as a decoy by her husband. Whenever he spots an interesting tramp, punk rocker, or skinhead, he quickly poses his wife near his subject and pretends to take her picture. By using this sneaky method he has managed to build up a large collection of close-up, unposed photographs of great British eccentrics.

When I walked into the shop to replace Jo-Ann, who had taken over during my lunch break, she whispered to me, "That woman who is at the back of the shop has put her hand in the window to look at some books and disturbed the window display".

Unfortunately, Jo-Ann must have passed on this information to me in a stage whisper. As soon as Jo-Ann had left the shop, a customer came up to me and said:

"THAT WOMAN is my wife!".

Two lady customers were complaining about the stress of Christmas shopping. A male customer said, "I find Christmas a stressful time too. You feel obliged to get drunk, whether you like it or not".

On returning to the shop this morning, I found a note from Andy, who had served in the shop for me yesterday, which read:

"Please ring John Major"

Had High Street Bookshop attracted its first celebrity customer?

When I rang John Major he turned out to be a local architectural engineer who wanted me to value an 1842 edition of Addision's *Knights Templar*.

A local college lecturer came in to buy some paperbacks to put in his saddle bag. The college term has finished today and he leaves tomorrow for a cycling holiday in the Pyrenees.

The lecturer told me of his experiences on a similar holiday last year. On his journey through the mountains he was mugged by a rather large Spaniard who was wealding an axe. This year his saddle bag will contain defensive weapons as well as books!

I empathised with my customer's need for immediate escape at the end of the academic year. When I was a headteacher, I would make a getaway to the Continent on the very day on which term ended. After conducting the final staff meeting, I would walk to the foot of the school drive where Jo-Ann would be waiting with car and caravan. Some nine hours later we would be in France.

Last week a customer ordered Leary's *Psychedelic Experience,* Stafford's *Psychedelics Encyclopedia* and Schutte's *Plants of the Gods*. I did not question him too closely.

This week I discovered that my customer is a police officer who is carrying out research into the drug culture as part of his professional duties.

A former college lecturer from Kingston came into the shop this morning. He told me that he is researching a book about the history of flag days and charity collections.

We embarked on a conversation about the need for charity collections and we went on to discuss the current under-funding of education. I explained that I used to rely, as a headteacher, on the £10,000 raised annually by my P.T.A. to supplement the meagre budget allocated to my school.

Perhaps I should have organised an annual flag day!

A visitor from France asked if I could recommend a novel which would introduce him to the very best of English contemporary writing.

I had no hesitation in recommending Anita Brookner's *Hotel du Lac*, a book whose every adjective seems to have been selected with care and precision.

See Our
Great Titles

The *Bookseller* magazine gives an annual award to the most bizarrely named book of the year. Winners include: *The Book of Marmalade: its Antecendants, History and Role in the World Today; The Second International Workshop on Nude Mice* and *How to Shit in the Woods - an Environmentally Sound Approach to a Lost Art.* This year's winner is *Re-using Old Graves* by D. Davies and A. Shaw.

Books with some wonderfully bizarre titles find their way into my shop from time to time. My current favourites are:

* *Gay Bulgaria*
(When this book was written, Bulgaria was anything but gay and the word "gay" had not yet acquired its modern meaning!)

*   *Dreams about H M the Queen* by Brian Masters.
(Sigmund Freud would have enjoyed this one!)

*   *Doing up a Dump* by Barty Phillips.
(I placed this book in the window, and inserted a bookmark which bore the legend: "SEE OUR GREAT TITLES")

* *High Level Wellness* by Donald B Ardell.
(Although the title suggests a medical guide for aircraft passengers, the sub-title claims that the book contains advice which is *An Alternative to Doctors, Drugs and Disease*)

* *How not to Kill Your Husband* by a Family Doctor.
(Brings to mind Basil Fawlty's favourite film, *How to Murder your Wife*)

* *The Year of the Cornflake* by Faith Addis.
(I wonder if this story has been "cerealised"?)

400 Local Authors

According to a recent B.B.C. television poll, one person in ten thinks they could write a book and one in fifty has already done so. On the basis of these findings, Buxton, a town of some 20,000 people, is home to no less than 400 authors!

Only a handful of Buxton's writers are published authors. Writing a book is difficult enough, but getting a finished manuscript accepted for publication is far, far more difficult. Some 88,000 books are published annually in this country - a seemingly enormous number of volumes, and large indeed when compared to the output in many other countries, but only a tiny fraction of the books which are sent to publishing houses each year.

Most writers who submit their scripts to publishers experience a succession of dispiriting rejections, and not necessarily because their work isn't worthy of publication. Publishers often make mistakes;

occasionally they are guilty of enormous errors of judgement. One of the novels which was shortlisted for the 1994 Booker Prize - Jill Paton Walsh's *Knowledge of Angels* - was published at the author's own expense after it had been rejected by a string of publishers.

Some local writers who are unable to find a publisher for their work follow the example of Ms Paton Walsh and resort to self-publishing. Some are lucky enough to make a small profit; most never recoup their expenses. Other local authors turn in desperation to vanity publishers, often using their life savings in order to realise a life-long ambition to see their work in print. The desire to be published has a great deal to do with our need to cheat death. Authors achieve immortality through their books: their best thoughts live on in neatly-bound volumes long after they have passed away.

The Peak District contains a number of small publishing houses, such as Bob Mulholland`s Caron Publications, John Merrill`s Footprint Press and Dr Mitchell`s Scarthin Publications, which help local authors into print, but Buxton is unique in having a minister of the church who is also a publisher. Reverend Bob Davies, Minister of Buxton Methodist Church, has set up a little publishing house, Church in the Market Place Publications, for the benefit of local writers. Here is one minister who can give a genuine guarantee of immortality to members of his flock!

As a bookseller, I am always delighted to promote books by local writers. My motives are not entirely altruistic: local authors become local celebrities and signed copies of their books are much sought after by local people.

Terry Lamsley writes tales of supernatural terror which are set in and around Buxton.

"Why do I have this compulsion to fill an innocent, harmless little town like Buxton with all kinds of horrors?" says Terry. "Better not to ask, I guess".

Terry crossed my path as I walked along Broad Walk this morning. Emerging from a passageway between two large Victorian villas, he looked like a ghostly character from one of his stories. He walked into the Pavilion Gardens and then disappeared eerily into the morning mist.

One customer told me that he had found a footprint on a manuscript which had been returned to him by a publisher.

This tale may be apocryphal but it does illustrate the frustration which is felt by so many aspiring writers.

Twelve "vanity publishers" who were the subject of a 1994 survey brought out an average of sixty titles each and sold just six copies per title.

Maureen Allen brought in copies of her little book about the Peak District village of Cressbrook. The book is self-published, and Maureen has done a wonderful job on publicity. She has produced posters, given radio and television interviews and distributed press-releases to local newspapers. She has also organised a book-launch at Cressbrook Hall.

Maureen's energetic approach is an object lesson for would-be authors and a clear demonstration that self-publishing is a much better option than vanity publishing.

Maureen is an ex-teacher and a former resident of Cressbrook. She now lives at Caldbeck, in the Lake District. Her book contains acknowledgements to Chris and Wendy Bonington and their son Rupert, her near neighbours in Cumbria. Rupert helped with the photographs and Chris sent the following message to the launch:

"Altogether a delightful piece of local history which I am sure that the people of Cressbrook and all who visit it, will value. It gives an extra dimension of understanding to this quiet Derbyshire dale. I only wish that I could have been here to share in the launch, and go and grab a climb in Ravensdale to finish".

I attended the launch party at the Palace Hotel for Mike Langham and Colin Wells' book *Robert Rippon Duke, The Architect of Victorian Buxton*. Councillors, Council officers, librarians (the book has been published by Derbyshire Library Service), booksellers, local authors and members of Buxton's Archaeological Society were all there to celebrate the publication of a book which has been seven years in the writing.

R.R.D, as the authors affectionately dub their subject, was a prolific architect who did much to enhance the face of Buxton. Among his lesser-known works are the town's elaborate Victorian lamp-posts.

Higher Buxton traders have just contributed £500 towards the cost of fixing hanging baskets to the lamp-posts which line the High Street. Bob Hall told me today that it would not be possible to decorate all the posts. The town's modern lamp standards cannot take the strain of hanging baskets. Only the R.R.D. lamp-posts are strong enough to hold the metal baskets.

So much for engineering progress!

Bob Davies has asked me to proof read the manuscript of Harry Swindell's latest book of reminiscences about life in the Peak District village of Chelmorton. Harry gives a fine portrait of a bygone era. In one passage he describes his daily two-mile walk across the White Peak from Chelmorton to Millers Dale station, where he caught the train to his school in Bakewell.

Today's parents would not take the risk of allowing their child to make a solo walk through lonely countryside. Come to think of it, today's children would not contemplate making such a walk either - they would demand a lift in the family car.

How times have changed!

David Owen, the gargantuan author of *The Old Road to Fairfield*, promised to let me have further copies of his popular book. He told me that he would not be bringing in the books himself, as he would find it difficult to get through the small doorway of the shop. A friend would bring them in.

I was talking to Katie, an ex-colleague from the world of education, when Mike Langham came into the shop with some copies of Langham and Wells' book *Six Buxton Gentlemen*.

Katie is the most liberated of ladies, and Mike was quick to read the expression on her face when she spotted the title of his book. Pre-empting her comments, Mike expressed regret that so few women had been able to reach eminent positions in Victorian Buxton.

An article in this week's *Buxton Advertiser* lists "Mike Smith's Bookshop" as one of the places where David Owen's book on Fairfield can be purchased. Throughout this week customers have been coming into the shop and asking, "Are you Mike Smith and do you have a copy of *The Old Road to Fairfield*?"

I feel like Lobby Ludd must have felt when readers of the Daily Mirror came up to him and said, "You are Lobby Ludd and I claim my £1,000".

Sheila and Howard have been over to stay this weekend. On Sunday morning we took them to the Goyt Valley where we walked from Errwood reservoir to the ruins of Errwood Hall. By coincidence, Gerald Hancock came into the shop today (Monday) with copies of his new book, *The Goyt Valley and its People*. The book contains vivid descriptions of the hall and the Grimshawe family who lived there. I am delighted to read that the Grimshawes were great bibliophiles. Books lined the study and the upstairs sitting room, and there were eleven more cupboards of books in the house!

My first in-shop signing session took place today. Harry Swindell was in the shop to sign copies of *What a Life - and More Poetry*. This is Harry's third book of poems and reminiscences. All three books have been published by Rev. Bob Davies' Church in the Market Place publishing house. Harry told me that Bob had "plucked him from obscurity" in 1994 by publishing his first book, *In His Grass Roots*. Harry was 88 years old at the time!

Harry Swindell signs copies of What a Life - and More Poetry.

According to today's *Telegraph*, Susan Hill is joining the ranks of distinguished modern authors who are self-publishing their work. Jill Paton Walsh and Timothy Mo have both resorted to self-publishing novels which did not find favour with publishers. Walsh's revenge on publishers was complete when her book made the Booker Prize shortlist! Susan Hill's motives seem to be rather different - she has taken as her inspiration Virginia Woolf's Hogarth Press, a highly successful cottage industry.

I sent the cutting from the *Telegraph* to Maureen Allen, author of *Cressbrook*. Maureen runs her own cottage industry, which includes publishing and craft products, in the Lake District.

I was asked to market a periodical which is produced by a local writers' group. The magazine's editor contributes a question-and-answer advice column for wannabe writers. The column includes the following:

Q.   I wish I could write like you - but I'm not intelligent enough: My spelling's dreadful and I'm forever getting my words muddled up.

A.   I believe that one is entitled to a little poetic license (sic) Don't let the so-called intellects (sic) drag you down. Writing can be a lonely pass-time. (sic)

Trevor Hall, a retired postman from Tideswell, came in with copies of his self-published novel, *Sugarcups and Daisies*. As it was a quiet day in the shop (largely as a result of the appalling weather) I settled down to read the book. Trevor's novel spans the century and follows the fortunes of Tideswell families in war and peace. The author has a fine feel for the rhythm of life on the harsh limestone plateau of the Peak and a deep understanding of the nature of friendship. He also betrays a very romantic nature.

Trevor's well-written book deserves to have a publisher other than himself.

Alan Watson, the author of *Bygone Days of Chinley*, has been invited to put on a display of old photographs in the Hearse House Visitor Centre in Chapel-en-le-Frith. I met Alan at the visitor centre to help him mount the exhibition.

Alan showed me a wonderful photograph of a group of eighteen prim and proper ladies from the Chinley Liberal Club. The photograph is captioned "Lady Members of the Chinley Liberal Party visiting Glossop, 1915". Alan told me that he had toyed with the caption "The Liberal Ladies of Chinley", before deciding that this would be just a little too naughty!

David Owen's self-published local history book, *The Old Road to Fairfield*, has sold out very quickly, not only in my shop, but also in all other local bookshops. Having paid a considerable sum for a print run of 500 copies, David is understandably reluctant to risk further expenditure, but the long waiting list of people who would like to purchase the book suggests that a second print run is needed.

If further copies are not produced, the book will soon become a collector's item, with copies changing hands in second-hand bookshops (like mine) at greatly inflated prices.

Today's *High Peak Reporter* carries a story about Rosie Fellows, a former mill worker from Whaley Bridge who has written a novel called *Weaver's Knot*. Rosie is looking for a publisher.

Rosie came into my shop last week to ask my advice about publication.

It strikes me that would-be artists have it so much easier than would-be authors. Anyone who paints a picture can frame their work at little expense and then hang it or even offer it for sale, but most would-be authors are denied the satisfaction of seeing their work in published form.

Gerald Hancock's book, *Goyt Valley and its People,* contains a photograph of a shooting party at the gatehouse of Errwood Hall. The photograph is very carefully staged. The nine men in the party have been posed in such a way that only one of them is actually looking at the camera; most are sitting sideways on, some facing left, others looking to the right - each member of the group looks totally detached from every other member of the group.

This peculiar picture brings to mind an incident at one of our favourite restaurants in the South of France. The waiter at this restaurant has a most disconcerting habit: he never makes eye-to-eye contact when he serves up a dish - as he extends his hand to the left with a plate, he turns his face and his gaze to the right. On one occasion, the inevitable happened - our meal was delivered to the wrong table. As soon as we realised that the people at the next table were tucking into our chosen dish, we called for the waiter. Fawlty-like, he snatched the plates from under the startled diners, rushed to the kitchen with the meal, flicked off any partially-eaten morsels, turned round immediately, and brought the meal to our table!

Dr. Joyce Critchlow gave me a picture-postcard of King Sterndale

Church for my pin-board. I gave Joyce a signed copy of my guidebook to Chapel-en-le-Frith. Joyce gave me a signed copy of her book *Recipes from a Rectory Kitchen*.

Today I wrote to Joyce to say how much I had enjoyed her recipe book.

The book is not only a collection of healthy and natural homecooking recipes, but also a month-by-month account of life in a Peak District village. It reads like a delightful Derbyshire version of Peter Mayle's *A Year in Provence*.

Joyce is very good on the Peak District winter:

"Here, in the Derbyshire Peak District, it's a fair assumption that whatever Candlemas brings, winter will have at least another flight".

"While the TV screen shows London trees still in leaf at the Remembrance Day Cenotaph service, ours have long since fallen and are on the compost heaps".

Joyce also describes a number of trips beyond the boundaries of the Peak District, including visits which she made to Yorkshire with her mother, who was born and bred in the county. Her account of their outings past the great West Yorkshire rhubarb fields, which have "now given way to industrial sites and/or motorways", brought back memories of the Sunday afternoon cycle rides which I made as a young teenager from my home in Leeds to nearby villages. Our picnic stop was always taken in a lay-by close to the Tingley rhubarb fields. The area is now occupied by an out-of-town commercial and entertainment centre. Rhubarb has given way to Big Macs!

Joyce's culinary references to Yorkshire naturally include descriptions of Yorkshire Puddings: she recalls that the products of her mother's first attempts at making Yorkshire Pudding were described as "leather waistcoats" by Joyce's grandfather. This anecdote brought to mind a story from my own early days in Yorkshire:

One of our neighbours in Leeds sought a divorce from his wife largely on the grounds that she was incapable of making acceptable Yorkshire Puddings!

When Joyce gave me the signed copy of *Recipes from a Country Rectory*, she told me about a typographical error in the book - the name of one of the Ladies of the vale, at Plas Newydd, North Wales, has been printed as Parsonby rather than Ponsonby. Authors are always upset about printing errors in their published work, but I suggested to Joyce that she should not worry unduly about this particular mistake. The spelling "Parsonby" is entirely appropriate for a book which was written in a country rectory!

They Said It

Publishers decorate the dust-jackets of their books with carefully-selected quotes from favourable reviews; theatrical impressarios plaster their billboards with hyperbolical statements from supportive critics; I decorate my bookshop with quotations from well known bibliophiles.

"Even bad books are books and therefore sacred".

Gunter Grass

"The sight of a shelf of books - any books - fills me with respect. To know that I can return home at the end of a day, which may contain more distress that gratification, and open a book, is a very present confirmation that life is worth living.".

Anita Brookner

"It is good to live in a world where bookshop assistants like books, rather than one where they don't care whether they are selling books or cornflakes".

Tom Stoppard

"There's still something to be said for books, don't you think? For example, there is the way a writer and his reader don't have to meet. So the writer can compose his voice. Though hesitant, he can become swift; though shy, dashing. So the reader can suit himself, too. If bored, he can speed up or skip; if interested or puzzled, he can go back, slow down or pause".

David Sexton

(This passage sums up perfectly the special quality of books and the joy of reading).

"They imagined books would make them less shy and (always an ambition) able to "mix". Quiet and never particularly gregarious, they cherished a life-long ambition to "branch out", with books somehow the key to it".

Alan Bennett
writing about his parents in "Writing Home".

"It had always been obvious to me that anyone in England wanting to become knowledgeable or cultured, no matter what their income or status, could do so freely, and at little cost. They still can.

Libraries are free, second-hand books almost given away, and a basic radio will provide familiarity with classical music".

Alan Sillitoe

"The oldest books are only just out to those who have not read them".

Samuel Butler

"Books do furnish a room".

Anthony Powell

(A recent newspaper photograph of Powell shows the author reclining, in aristocratic pose, on the chaise longue in his book-lined study).

"If a book is worth reading it is worth buying".

John Ruskin

(An excellent motto for a bookshop. However, it might be worth adding: "If a book is worth buying it is worth reading". I wonder just how many books are bought, simply because they are fashionable or furnish a room, but never actually read)

"She read Rimbaud, the French symbolists, the Dadaists, Lewis

Carroll, William Blake, Roland Barthes, Swift; she plunged into medieval texts, Chaucer, Boccaccio. She discovered glum realists (like Philip Larkin), but loved the satirists and tale spinners and fabulists; the writers who distrusted "naturalness" and for whom decadence was not a dirty word. She liked dizzying, topsy-turvy worlds, where reality was on the surface and illusion within".

Nicci Gerard
writing about the novelist Angela Carter.

"I have been a hopeless addict of second-hand bookshops ever since my schooldays".

Denis Healey

(The photograph on the dust-jacket of Denis Healey's *My Secret Planet* shows Denis, dressed in a comfortable cardigan, sitting with an open book on his lap, in front of a bookshelf which is crammed with fine volumes).

The Coldest Place
in England

During the final seventeen years of my teaching career I made a daily journey across the Peak District from my home in the High Peak to my school in Sheffield. On a good day the journey would take about thirty-five minutes; on a bad day, with heavy snow falling on the White Peak plateau, the same journey could take up to three hours.

Many is the time I have been met by the incredulous stares of colleagues as I have staggered up the front steps of the school. "I thought Buxton was cut off", they would say. "According to this morning's radio bulletin, all roads out of the town are blocked".

I only failed to complete my journey on two occasions in all those years, but I had some horrific and nerve-racking experiences in the snowfields of Derbyshire.

I no longer have to make those daily journeys, but I still have my battles with the Peak District weather.

There are many days in the year when Buxton is the coldest place in England. At such times, my shop, which stands on the perimeter of Buxton's exposed Market Place, and some 1,000 ft above sea-level, is subject to the full force of the Arctic winds.

A June day in Buxton ?!

I rang a bookdealer in Colchester today. When I told him that I was calling from Buxton, he said, "Isn't that the place where it's always snowing?"

Customers who come into the shop to buy Stuart Whatley's *Arctic Buxton* often supply me with anecdotes about the famous winter of 1947:

One customer told me that she had been stopped by the police for sledging down the middle of Fairfield Road.

Another customer gave me his version of the famous 1947 airlift of food to isolated farms on the White Peak Plateau. Eight men were killed when an R.A.F. Dakota crashed during the airlift operation. According to Stuart's book, local residents were "angry that airmen who had survived the war should die like that". My customer told me of a different reaction. He said that the people who lived on the moor had been angry that anyone should think it necessary to drop supplies to Peakland farmers who were always well-prepared for any eventuality.

I put out a pavement A-board for the first time this morning. Ten minutes later it was blown over by the wind.

Today I bought several copies of old *Buxton Guidebooks* for the shop.

The 1936 edition of the *Buxton Guidebook* describes Buxton as "the Spa of the Blue Waters", and contains the following eulogy:

"An altitude of 1,000 ft, with a consequent tonic and invigorating climate, an air of unsurpassed purity and dryness".

As I read this, the rain was lashing against the window of the shop and the wind was blowing so hard that my pavement A-board was in danger of becoming airborne again!

This morning I cursed and swore as I made my fourth attempt to de-ice the shop window which was completely frozen over after a dreadfully cold January night.

A regular customer, who was passing the shop during this operation, opened the door and told me that he had just learnt some new swear words from me.

When I had finally managed to clear the ice from the window, I went across to the post office for some stamps. The postmaster said, "Weren't the ice patterns on your shop window beautiful this morning?"

Copies of Ian Currie's book *Frosts, Freezes and Fairs* arrived today. The book contains the following statistics about Buxton's weather:

1947 Snow on the ground for 71 days in Buxton.
1979 Snow on the ground for 83 days!
1985 Temperature only crept above freezing point for a few hours in the entire month of February.

The book also contains a splendid photograph taken in Buxton in January 1987. A resident opens her bedroom window to grasp the huge icicles which are hanging from the guttering of her house.

A customer bought a copy of *In the Wake of the Hurricane* for her sister in Folkestone (the book contains photographs of the devastation that followed the 1987 hurricane which swept southern counties). She told me that her sister, who had been woken by the sound of the hurricane, had watched from her bedroom window as the roof of the terrace of houses across the street was ripped off by the force of the gale.

It's raining in Buxton today. The weather forecasters predicted snow in their bulletin this morning. Ever since they failed to predict the Great Hurricane of 1987, the weather-forecasters have been playing safe by making over-alarmist forecasts. If they do ever predict another hurricane, no-one will take their forecast seriously!

I noticed in a *Guinness Book of Records* that the lowest recorded temperature in England is 11 degrees Fahrenheit (43 degrees of frost) - recorded at Buxton in 1895!

K. C. Edward's book *The Peak District* contains some depressing weather statistics for Buxton:

Meteorological records between 1928 and 1954 show that the town has an average of 38 days of snow per year and 211 days when there is some rainfall. During this 32 year period there was an average of only 3.3 hours of sunshine per day (some 27% of total daylight hours). Put another way, in Buxton it is almost three times as likely to be dull as sunny!

However, we do have some consolation - on a clear, sunny day, there is nowhere quite like Buxton. The grey stonework on the town's grand and elegant buildings takes on a warm brown hue; the limestone hills to the south of the town, which can look so dull and forbidding on an overcast day, are softened by the light grey of the walls and the pastel-green of the fields; the gritstone hills to the north form a dark silhouette against a clear blue sky.

A customer bought a book on Antarctica for her son who had been away on a three-year polar expedition - his base in Antarctica was a seashore location in the summer, but 100 miles from the sea in the winter when the ocean froze over. She told me that her son had done his survival training in preparation for Antarctica at Corbar Rocks in Buxton. Our somewhat extreme climate does have its uses!

Buxton vies with Alston, in Cumbria, for the honour of being Britain's highest market town.

Regardless of any altitude statistics, Buxton must have the most exposed market place in the country. Today's wet and windy weather has decimated the number of stalls on the Saturday market and, consequently, the number of Saturday visitors to High Street Bookshop.

On one famous June day in 1975 "Snow stopped Play" at the Buxton's County Cricket Ground.

I looked through the collection of *Wisdens* on the shelves of my bookshop for accounts of other County matches at Buxton, and found the following depressing entries:

Derbyshire vs Sussex - August 1961
"Play was possible only on the first day because of rain".
Derbyshire vs Somerset - July 1959
First day - "rain interfered seriously with play"
Second day - "rain washed out the second day"
Then - "Further rain ended the game".
Derbyshire vs Lancashire - June 1957
"Rain seriously curtailed play"

Little wonder that the ground is no longer used for County matches!

A customer bought a copy of Stuart Whatley's *Arctic Buxton* to send to her daughter who is a meteorologist with the U.S. Airforce. My customer told me of the period which she had spent in the real Arctic, in Anchorage, Alaska with her U.S. serviceman husband. At midnight in mid-summer they would stand on the veranda of their quarters and watch the sun skim the horizon. The winter nights were far less romantic: even a combination of central heating and blow-heaters could not maintain their room at a tolerable temperature - conditions not dissimilar to those in High Street

Bookshop last December!

It is July lst today, but the temperature in Buxton is such that I have had to turn on the shop's calor gas heater!

Even Bad Books are Books

Some books change the course of history; most books reflect the age in which they were written. The fashions, beliefs, hopes and fears of an age are revealed in the pages of any book, fact or fiction.

Gunter Grass once said, "Even bad books are books and therefore sacred". Students of human development should certainly show due reverence for bad books, for they provide an uncensored guide to the history of human prejudices.

There is no better place in which to study the true history of the Twentieth Century than in a second-hand bookshop.

Bibby's Annual for 1911 contains an article entitled *Fundamental Causes of Unemployment and Some Suggestions Thereupon.*

The author (who hides behind the nom de plume "Musicus") makes his feelings very clear in his opening sentence:

"Without doubt largely, if not entirely, the real underlying cause of unemployment is to be found in the physical and mental unfitness of the unemployed themselves, who, although apparently in happy ignorance of the fact, are so deficient in vitality and forceful energy as to be invariably almost entirely unemployable".

Musicus continues: "Unemployment is a product of the desire to live in ease and do as little work as possible".

"The unemployed should not be allowed to stand about idle, as it seriously aggravates the disease of inertia from which they are evidently suffering, and at the same time contaminates all others in the immediate vicinity". In Musicus' opinion, an unemployed man who is the father of the family should stay at home and take the place of the mother in caring for the children and the home, so freeing his wife to fill "one of the many vacancies for women servants". Musicus suggests that Labour exchanges should set aside a room where the unemployed should be put through a daily routine of physical and vocal exercises, to "strengthen their muscles and backbone, raise their spirits, and give them the nerve necessary to undertake any kind of work which might be offered them". He would teach the unemployed to sing - "after an hour of singing, see if you have not changed your flabby, inert and devitalised unemployed into a man - alert, upright, fit and energetic".

On yer bike!!!

During a few idle moments this morning, I tried a couple of exercises in *Little Children of the Great Round World,* a book which was published for schoolchildren in about 1920.

Question 1:   In what ways are the people of Italy like the people of Spain?

On checking the text, I found that "Spanish folk love to loll in the sunshine" and that "they are not fond of work", traits which are also attributed by the author to the Italians.

I also read that the young boys and girls of Italy "all love to dress in bright colours, even if they are in rags".

Question 2:   Which people, other than Moroccans, do not like strangers?

Before seeking an answer, I checked up on the Moroccans: "Not fond of seeing white men in their country. Indeed they often treat them rudely, and sometimes rob them of their money and goods".

The solution to my exercise was to be found in the chapter on Tibet: "It's people are an odd people. They do not wish to have anything to do with the folk of other lands".

I also discovered that "the children and the grown-ups are never washed. Indeed, nothing in Tibet is ever cleaned".

Just as I was about to tackle a third exercise Bob called in for a chat. I told him about the exercises which I had been tackling. Bob has just finished reading the copy of *Mein Kampf* which he had purchased from me last month.

We embarked on a long discussion about racial stereotyping.

Bob decided to buy *Little Children of the Great Round World* as a companion volume to *Mein Kampf*.

Alfred Bossom's *Building to the Skies* (1934) is a eulogy to the American skyscraper.

Bossom claims that the skyscraper is "perhaps America's greatest permanent contribution to any of the arts". He writes of the "soaring loveliness" of the Woolworth and Empire State buildings and suggests that "the Renaissance would not have disowned them". Bossom even praises a skyscraper hospital block in New York as "taking advantage of the pure air of the sky".

Should I reserve this book for the day when Prince Charles wanders into my shop?

Clarke's Second Law states: "If a well-known scientist states that something cannot be done, he is almost certain to be wrong".

There is ample proof of this little-known scientific law in the pages of *Modern Inventions* by V. E. Johnson M.A. (published about 80 years ago). Despite an assertion on page 165 that "to endeavour to look into the future is perhaps never wise", the author ventures a number of predictions:

"Save only for very special work, the aeroplane appears to have no particular future save as a military machine".

"The airship is an inherently stable machine".

"To compete with railways the aircraft would have to travel at between 120 and 150 mph. Undoubtedly, this could be done, but at what cost?"

"That man will ever be able to quit the earth and travel across interstellar space, say even to the moon, appears physically impossible".

"Those countries which possess vast deposits of peat will rapidly come to the front from the commercial point of view".

I came across a copy of *Emigrating to South Africa 1970-71,* compiled by Barclays Bank.

The principal message in this book is that white Europeans contemplating emigration to South Africa could look forward to a prosperous lifestyle and need have no worries about perceived threats from the black hordes.

The South African government's economic masterplan in 1970 rested on the development of new industries near the Bantu Homelands which would use unskilled labour and provide training for specific work. The aim was to encourage the Bantu population to concentrate itself on traditional areas. Unskilled labour in cities would then be replaced by mechanisation and automation.

In fact, the thirty photographs of South Africa used in this book create a strong impression that this separation of races had already been achieved. Not one of the illustrations features a non-white person. (Some care must have gone into their selection, as whites made up just 19% of the population of South Africa in 1970!)

Just in case the intending emigrant should still have worries about possible encounters with black or coloured people who might venture into White territory, he is given some reassuring character assessments-

The Bantu generally are 'cheerful and courteous'.

Cape coloureds are 'intelligent, humorous and pert, after the Cockney fashion, and are cheerful, colourful and musical'.

The Woman You Want To Be, Margery Wilson's "Complete Book of Charm", published during World War II, contains some very useful advice for ladies:

"You must have a goal - whether it is a husband, the learning of a language, a civil defence job, or public service".

"Pretty gestures used wisely will help you further your cause".

"Be careful of voicing opinions. The charming woman does not air hers freely".

"A clever woman I know says that she allows herself only two stated opinions during an evening. Needless to say, conversation around her is spirited and usually lasts for hours and hours. People love to go to her house".

"Pause in a doorway for an instant on entering a room anywhere, anytime. It gives you an opportunity to show yourself as a framed picture".

"Inane chatter is sometimes useful. Busy men find it restful, amusing".

"Manliness degenerates very quickly around women who provide no romantic flattery for masculine strength".

"Take a man on long walks - play golf with him - but always let him excel. On a long hike, be sure you get tired first".

"Never expect a man to fit in with your moods. You must fit into his".

Yesterday a customer who was about to face a selection test for a new job asked me for a book of intelligence tests. I supplied her with a copy of *Know Your Own IQ* by Professor Eysenck.

I then found myself slipping into teacher mode and giving her a series of product warnings:

* IQ tests include a time-limit, but "good thinking" is not necessarily "quick thinking".

* IQ test scores are a measure of average intelligence, but human abilities are often very specific.

*   Many IQ questions test "knowledge", rather than "intelligence".

The customer interrupted my flow and pointed out that I should be directing this stream of criticism at the employers who were about to judge her suitability for a job on the basis of her IQ test score.

Today, my customer called in the shop to let me know how she had got on: She hadn't got the job, and the tests which she had taken bore little resemblance to the questions in the Eysenck book which I had recommended to her.

At that moment, I felt like a teacher who has just scanned through the examination paper and discovered that he has been following the wrong syllabus with his pupils.

Towards Maturity, a Handbook for Older Girls, published in 1962 by the Sisters of Notre Dame, contains some useful advice for couples who plan to marry:

The sisters suggest that couples involved in long engagements should plan interesting and absorbing occupations, together and with other young people, so as to avoid too many and too prolonged occasions of possible strain and temptation in each other's exclusive company.

The book also contains advice for newly-weds: Honeymoons should be no more than a fortnight in length so as to minimise the risk of boredom.

Unsolicited Testimonials

Before we opened for business in September 1995 I put together some copy for an advertisement in the local paper. The text included the following "mission statement":

Mike hopes to create a little shop which will appeal to "all people who love books". He will be selling secondhand books on all subjects, collectable books, and a selection of new books at bargain prices. The shop will contain a large collection of popular fiction in paperback, and young readers will have their very own "Children's Corner".

Mike believes many bookshops are unfairly treated as "no-go" areas by particular groups of buyers. He says: "people who only buy new books miss out on the treasures waiting to be discovered in secondhand bookshops; if serious book collectors took the trouble to look in bargain bookshops they could well make unexpected finds; and, sadly, many children think bookshops are boring and unattractive places". Mike is keen to welcome buyers from all these groups into his shop.

Buxton's new bookseller says, "there are good bookshops in the town already, but he hopes that his shop will be a welcome addition to the Higher Buxton shopping area."

So much for the grand aims. What about the reality?

Mission statements must be followed up by evaluation (all the best business courses insist upon it) and I soon realised that I had at my disposal a very ready means of evaluation: off-the-cuff remarks made by customers about my shop.

A customer spent some time in the shop this morning. She didn't buy a book, but on her way out of the shop, she said, "Thank you for the music. I should like to have stayed longer".

Mozart's *Jupiter Symphony* was playing on the cassette.

A couple spent over half-an-hour in the shop, but left without buying a book. As they left, one said to the other, "I could spend hours in that shop".

Even though I had not made money from their visit, I was pleased by their comment. After all, the legend on my pavement A-board does say BROWSERS WELCOME.

A customer told me that he'd once been attracted into a bookshop in Manchester after spotting an interesting old encyclopedia in the shop window. Once inside the shop, he was surprised to find that the bookseller dealt exclusively in pornographic material.

Was my customer expressing dissatisfaction with the books on sale in my shop, or was he asking me to reach for the "special editions" under the counter?

An American tourist said to me, "I just love your bookstore".

I enjoyed the compliment, but I couldn't help wincing at the use of the word "bookstore" - a term which conjures up visions of some vast book supermarket, rather than a cosy little bookshop in Olde England.

Before coming into the shop, one couple had spent several minutes reading the notices and press cuttings in the doorway. They had paid particular attention to the cutting which describes my retirement from the headship of Silverdale School. As they left the shop, after a good ten minutes of browsing, one turned to the other and said, "That bookshop looks just like a headmaster's study".

Joe Tierney came into my shop today. Joe is a former HMI who inspected my school a few years ago. He now runs an antiquarian bookshop in Castleton.

Whilst Joe was looking around the shop I felt just as nervous as I had done during Joe's inspection of my school.

Peak Press' advertisement in the local paper for their *1997 Nostalgic Buxton Calendar* lists the stockists:

Buxton Advertiser	-	Market Place
Hargreaves	-	Spring Gardens
Mike Smith Books	-	High Street
Caron Publications	-	Chapel-en-le-Frith
Devonshire Library	-	The Colonnade
Country Bookstore	-	Cavendish Arcade

In the weeks before the bookshop opened, we toyed with several possible names for our new business - *Bookends, Bookworm, A Good Read, Top Shelf,* etc. After much discussion, we chose the unimaginative title *High Street Bookshop*, in the hope that this simple name would be easy to remember and would help fix the location of the shop in the minds of potential customers.

We now realise that many visitors to Buxton, and even some locals, think of Spring Gardens (the main shopping street in the spa area) as the town's High Street, and this latest newspaper advertisement is the second occasion on which a publisher has used the name *Mike Smith's Bookshop*, rather than *High Street Bookshop*. So much for our simple, memorable name!

American lady customer:

"I just love the way you arrange the books in your store. I'd love you to come to my house and re-arrange my shelves".

If these remarks had been made by Mae West they would have been construed as innuendo!

A colleague from my teaching days paid a visit to the shop with her mother. As she left the premises she said to her mother, "Rachel's description of Mike's bookshop was spot-on: the place really is very Dickensian".

Vivaldi's *Four Seasons* was playing on the cassette when a Canadian couple came into the shop. They told me that the same music was played at their local bookshop in Ontario.

My son Andy spotted a photograph of the Flatiron Building, New York, on the pin-board next to my serving desk. He pointed out that the end-on view of the skyscraper bears an uncanny resemblance to the facia of High Street bookshop!

High Street Bookshop and the Flatiron Building in New York.

Customers are always surprised to learn that I am not driven to insanity by the persistent bleeping of the pelican crossing outside my shop window. Normally, I am totally unaware of the noise, but today, I heard every bleep - the bleeper has just been repaired after two days of silence.

The human ear is immune to everyday background noise, but very alive to any change in sound.

A customer gave me a card which contained the following inscription:

"Thank you for taking the time to find the book for me. It was very much appreciated".

Two ladies came into the shop to buy some paperback fiction. As they left, one said to the other: "When you go into a shop like that, you realise just how much you have read".

I didn't quite know what to make of this comment. Was it a criticism of the small size of my stock?

The day began well:

My first customers were a couple from Bath. As he left the shop the man turned to his wife and said, "What a lovely bookshop".

A little later I overheard a remark made by another tourist as he looked in the shop window: "That's a lovely bookshop, that is".

I was brought back down to earth this afternoon:

As she was leaving the shop one customer asked me, "Could you tell me where I could find other junk shops in the town?"

Fair Exchange

A conversation about books often leads to an exchange of books.

Before the bookshop opened, I made a resolution: not one of the 2,000 books in my private collection would find its way on to the shelves of my bookshop. Although I cannot bear to part with any of my own books, I am only too willing to loan them to other bibliophiles in exchange for one of their recommended titles. Book-lovers like to share their enthusiasms.

Local people often bring in for my inspection books which are family heirlooms, other customers come along with ancient volumes which they have found in the attic and aspiring authors bring in their manuscripts.

To run a second-hand bookshop is to run a small literary club.

Michelle loaned me a book about the First World War cartoonist, Bruce Bairnsfather. In return, I loaned Michelle a collection of Dylan Thomas' poems, stories and essays.

Dylan Thomas suffers from verbal diarrhoea - the wonderful opening sentence of his essay on Laugharne contains no less than seven adjectives and over thirty nouns.

Bairnsfarther is able to sum up a situation and make a telling comment in just one illustration and a single caption.

Two very different geniuses!

I bought a collection of classic crime novels from a lady whose eyesight is now too poor for reading. She is using proceeds from the sale to buy books on audio-tape. I felt sorry for her, but she is grateful that she can continue her enjoyment of literature with the help of a little technology.

The collection which I bought from her includes a good batch of works by Edgar Wallace. My father was a great Edgar Wallace fan. He used to tell me that the author died from drinking too much tea. I have no idea where he got this story from, or how much truth there is in it!

A couple from Cornwall asked if I could recommend a meandering motor-route from Buxton to Harrogate which would give them a flavour of the North. I suggested: Buxton to Glossop, Glossop to Holmfirth via *Last of the Summer Wine* Country, Holmfirth to the Industrial Revolution settlements of Hebden Bridge and Heptonstall, Heptonstall to the model village of Saltaire and its gallery of David Hockney pictures, across the fringe of the Yorkshire Dales via the American spy station at Menwith Hill to Harrogate.

They bought a road atlas and gave me the address of a good campsite in Cornwall.

I had a long discussion about the Kennedy assassination with a customer who bought a book about the president's final days. She was full of praise for the film *J.F.K.* and said she would lend me the video of the film.

After watching the video I wrote the following notes:

"Very effective mix of technicolour acted sequences and black-and-white documentary footage. But a few of the acted sequences are filmed in black-and-white - this is unfair, as it gives these episodes undue factual weight."

"The CIA/Mafia/FBI/Cuba connections all ring true. I have always thought that Kennedy was killed by his own secret service in response to the secret deal which he struck with Kruschev at the time of the Cuban Missile Crisis. But I find it difficult to accept the premise that Kennedy wished to pull America out of Vietnam. Vietnam was Kennedy's worst legacy, and hung like a millstone round LBJ's neck."

63

"I have always thought that Oswald was a carefully manufactured scapegoat. Was he drugged? Was he paid? Was he hypnotised? Was he programmed?"

When I returned the video to the customer and handed her my notes, we engaged in further animated discussion. Another customer who was in the shop at the time suggested that I should set up a debating society in the shop. No need - I already have one!

Last week, I delivered a book to a Sheffield customer, Mike Gill, who gave me a conducted tour of his splendid collection of books on topography and local history.

Mike showed me an account of the life of A. E. Allen, the Sheffield Artist. We both admired a reproduction of Allen's painting of *Derbyshire Walls*. I sent Mike the following extract from my little Peak District guidebook:

"Just as a covering net accentuates the writhings of a trapped animal, so the stone walls of the Peak District pick out and exaggerate every change of contour: bumps are made into hills, potentially monotonous plains are shown to have interesting undulations and shallow valleys. And the stone walls cannot be described as an imposition on the landscape, for they are made of the very stuff on which they stand. To my eye at least, the Peak District is a landscape which is made interesting and attractive by its network of stone walls."

Today I received through the post from Mike a postcard of A. E.

Allen's painting. I blue-tacked the picture on the wall above my display of Peak District books.

Peak District walls.

Last week I had an experience which was out-of-this-world:

I looked at the moon through my newly-acquired telescope and saw the flat white disc which is so familiar to the naked eye transformed into a fantastic three-dimensional landscape. As I focused on three perfectly-circular, high-walled craters I felt as close to the moon as an astronaut in lunar orbit.

With the acquisition of a telescope, my fascination with Space, which began in childhood with the books of Patrick Moore and the exploits of Dan Dare and the Mekon, has been re-kindled.

Having bought me the telescope as a birthday present, Jo-Ann supplied star guides, a moon map and a planisphere as a Christmas gift.

A customer who came into the shop today told me that he had also recently acquired an astronomical telescope. He was on the look-out for guides to the stars and planets and maps of the heavens. I offered to let him see my own maps and star guides before he placed his order. He offered to loan me his collection of videos on astronomical topics.

It seems that Buxton has a brand new astronomy club with two very enthusiastic founder members!

Mike's study-cum-observatory in Chapel-en-le-Frith

How Much is That Doggie in the Window?

The curved, all-glass, Art Deco frontage of High Street Bookshop offers wonderful opportunities for theatrical window display.

In the months before we opened we were always on the look-out for suitable props for use in the window. I found some nice art-deco book-ends in an antique shop in Sheffield's Abbeydale Road and I also discovered some delicate, mock-Georgian book-ends in one of Sharrow Vale Road's antique shops; Jo-Ann unearthed her grandfather's reading glasses, my mother-in-law donated a magnifying glass and my sister-in-law persuaded the local Catholic church to loan us a beautiful brass lectern. I cut photographs out of newspapers and hunted through my collection of postcards for suitable illustrations.

Once we had opened, it did not take me long to realise that the shop window offers a powerful means of free advertising. Books which are displayed in the

window sell quickly, books on specialist topics which are placed in the window send out a message that there are other books on those subjects available inside the shop; any newly-published book on local history which is put on display immediately becomes a best-seller.

It was not long before I made another important discovery. When customers ask: "Is everything in the window for sale?", they are not simply referring to the books on display. I could have sold my book-ends, antique reading glasses, magnifying glass and the brass lectern many times over.

My window display includes a small framed photographic still life which I bought on the Rue de Rivoli, in Paris. The picture shows an antiquarian book and a bottle of old wine on the surface of a small antique table.

This little photograph is very simple but highly evocative - the viewer is left to imagine the book-lined study, the large easy-chair by the table, the occupant of the chair, and the evening of pleasure which the book and the wine will provide.

A couple asked me if they could buy the picture. I directed them to the Rue de Rivoli.

Val gave me a superb pair of book-ends in the shape of globes of the Earth. I shall use them in the window to display children's books. This splendid prop cost all of £1.00 in a discount store!

I bought a small wooden jewellery case in the shape of a book.

I put the open "book" in the window and placed inside it a card with the following caption:

"BOOKS ARE TREASURE CHESTS"

Two boys came in the shop and asked: "How much is that Book of Secrets in the window?"

A book which is currently on display in the window has a typical portrait by Modigliani on its front cover.

A father and son paused by the window. The father asked his son if he could identify the artist featured on the book. The son recognised the painter immediately, but had difficulty in pronouncing the artist's name correctly. After the boy had made three or four brave, but incorrect attempts, the father became impatient with him and pulled a long face - a face which bore a remarkable resemblance to the elongated image on the cover of the Modigliani book!

The "Holiday Reading" display in my shop window features a sun-hat, a copy of *France* magazine, a guide to Euro Disney and a polaroid camera.

A customer who had seen the window display came in to ask if I could advise her on the repair of a polaroid camera which she had purchased at a car boot sale!

A customer asked if she could purchase the brass lectern which I use in my window display. She explained that the lectern would be perfect as a base for the Edwardian picture album which holds her family photographs.

She was most disappointed when I explained that the lectern is on loan from a local church.

I obtained a laser print of one of Salvador Dali's best pieces of trickery - the painting, which is a rear view of Gala from close-up, transforms into a portrait of Abraham Lincoln when viewed from a distance. I placed the picture in the window and attached to it the following slogan:

ART BOOKS AT SURREAL PRICES

Last week I placed in the window a reproduction of Perugini's painting *Girl Reading*.

On a visit to Manchester Art Gallery this weekend I spotted the original version of the painting. A helpful description taught me a great deal about the picture:

The orange tree which is featured in the painting represents the Fall of Woman (a woman having plucked oranges from the Tree of Knowledge). According to legend, redemption can be found only by the reading of learned books, such as the one in the girl's hand.

Perhaps I should write a new caption for the picture in my window: "Women of Buxton - Come into High Street Bookshop and seek redemption!"

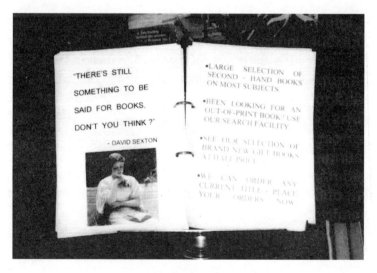

Perugini's 'Girl Reading' on display in the window.

I have placed Jo-Ann's grandfather's reading glasses on an open book in the window. They attracted the attention of a passing Beatles fan.

"How much are those John Lennon glasses in the window?" he asked.

The long school holiday is only a few days old, but "Back-to-School" promotions are already beginning to appear in the windows of school outfitters, stationers and bookshops. During my schooldays, firstly as a pupil and later as a teacher, I was always depressed by the sight of these cruel reminders that even the long summer vacations are finite.

Now, as a bookseller, I find myself upsetting passing students and teachers who have just begun their well-earned summer rest. I have even gone to the trouble of borrowing a mortar board from a former colleague, to lend weight to my window display of school text books.

Last week I acquired a vast collection of old school textbooks. I placed some of them in the window in a large pile, and then wrote out the slogan:

ARE YOU STUDYING FOR:
SATs
GCSE
A-LEVELS?
START YOUR REVISION HERE

A customer came in the shop today and said to me:

"Each time I have passed your shop in the last week I have tried to work out what on earth SATs might be. Can you put me out of my misery?"

After I had told him about the new Standard Attainment Tests, he said:

"The eleven-plus, O-levels and A-levels served us well in our day. Why tamper with a perfectly good system?"

I told my customer about the apartheid ceremony which took place on the day I received my eleven-plus result. I wrote the following description of the event in an essay which I produced for my graduate Certificate in Education:

"When the headmaster came into our classroom with the results he embarked on a very lengthy conversation with our form teacher before making any announcement to the class. Whilst the two teachers inspected the pass-list and exchanged knowing nods about our performance, we waited fretfully for news of our fate. We were seated, as always, in strict meritocratic order (as measured by our performance in the last set of school examinations): high-flyers in seats at the back left-hand corner of the room, dim-wits in the front right-hand corner by the door.

When the headmaster turned at last to speak to the class, he began his address by issuing firm instructions on the protocol to be followed during the receipt of our results. "I shall read out the names of all those pupils who have passed the eleven-plus examination," he said. "When your name is called, stand up by your desk, and remain standing." The pass-list was read out very slowly, and the successful candidates rose from their seats one-by-one. When the announcement was over, there was a short silence during which the unsuccessful candidates waited hopefully, but in vain, for more names to be called. When it became clear that the list was complete, those who had failed the examination burst into tears and fell, with their heads buried in their hands, on to their desk lids. We, the successful pupils, stood proudly by our desks and looked down on the failures."

A perfectly good system?

Mi-Amigo, David Harvey's new book about the American Flying Fortress which crashed in Endcliffe Park, Sheffield in 1944 has been selling well.

When I took delivery of a second batch of books, the publishers (ALD Design & Print) loaned me a model of a Flying Fortress for promotional purposes.

In the two days since I placed the model aircraft in the window I have sold no further copies of *Mi-Amigo*, however three customers have asked if they could buy the model.

Buxton in Books

Buxton is a place which is full of contradictions: the highest town in England, but set in a wooded hollow with soft river scenery; a health resort, but with a climate which only the fit and healthy can withstand; a grand and elegant town, but built in a style, and on a scale, foreign to the district.

The town's best building, the eighteenth century Crescent, occupies a sunken position at the foot of steep gardens, known as the Slopes, but when viewed from the summit of the Slopes, the Crescent sits centre-stage in a wonderfully theatrical townscape. In fact, Buxton has one of the finest townscapes in England, and the town is situated in the heart of some of Britain's best countryside. And yet Buxton does not always receive the recognition it deserves in travel literature and guidebooks.

The Shell Guide to England contains the following entry:

"Buxton is in the heart of impressive scenery, some of the best being seen by taking the minor road to the small villages of Peak Dale and Peak Forest to the north-east. Here you cross the roof of England, a wide, almost prehistoric landscape, criss-crossed with grey, drystone walls, here and there a hill rearing up, and the bareness relieved only by the occasional cluster of trees in a sheltered hollow, rarely enough to make a wood".

This description of the area around Peak Dale is highly poetic, but somewhat misleading.

Peak Dale is at the centre of large scale quarrying operations; its immediate surroundings are disfigured by some of the biggest quarries in Europe, and the tree clusters of the White Peak are found almost invariably not in hollows, but on hill tops, where they act as shelter-belts and prevent cattle from grazing on lead-polluted land!

The 1953 *Buxton Guidebook* contains a superb aerial view of Buxton's spa town. The photograph was probably taken from a helecopter as it passed over the Museum on Terrace Road, but the picture has been cleverly doctored by the superimposition, in the bottom right foreground, of a photograph of a limestone cliff. The viewer is left with the clear impression that a dramatic view of Buxton may be obtained from the summit of a precipitous limestone crag which stands above the town centre.

A very clever piece of gross misrepresentation - there are no limestone crags near the centre of Buxton!

Buxton from the crags! A rare view.

A war-time edition of the guidebook, claims that Buxton can offer "a holiday of peace in a safety zone". It also boasts the following statistics:

Normal population: 17,000
Population in the Season: 30,000

It is interesting to note that the corresponding figures in the 1953 guide are as follows:

Normal population: 19,556
Population in the Season: 23,000

A 74% drop in tourism in ten years??!

The churchwarden of the Arts and Crafts church on Dale Road dropped in, as promised, with a guide to the church.

The pamphlet contains some useful facts: the church was designed by Currey and Thompson; the angels on the corbels were carved by the Hunstones of Tideswell; and a horse called Fanny transported the building stone from Nithen End Quarry.

My 1973 copy of *Know Britain - The Heritage and Traditions of an Offshore Island* has the following one-line listing for Buxton under *Derbyshire Tourist Attractions:*

Buxton (Old Hall; Museum)

No mention of Buxton's greatest building - the Crescent! No mention of Buxton's greatest asset - the 26 acre Pavilion Gardens!

I acquired a copy of *Following the Fairways - A Companion to the Golf Courses of Great Britain*, published by Kensington West in 1987. The book contains a glowing tribute to Buxton:

"The Town of Buxton lies in the heart of the Peak District and is for many people their idea of the perfect town". I fully expected this introduction to be followed by the usual description of the town's fine Georgian and Victorian architecture, its splendid landscaped gardens and the nearby scenic attractions. However, the next sentence reads: "This may have something to do with the fact that some of the best pubs in England are located round about, but it is also helped by the fact that there are two excellent golf courses on either side of the town".

John Martin Robinson's *The Architecture of Northern England* contains a superb description of Buxton's spa town:

"The splendid Italianate and Francophile buildings have the feeling of being gathered together on the side of a mountain to make a Rex Whistler capriccio, rather than form a part of a real town".

Robinson's capriccio is best appreciated from the summit of the gardens known as the Slopes. I always recommend a visit to this vantage point to any tourists who come into my shop. All the grand and eccentric buildings of the spa are visible from this spot. They include the Italianate St. John's Church and the Chateau-like Palace Hotel. Robinson describes Higher Buxton, where my shop is located, thus:

"The old market town, with its funnel-shaped Market Place, humble old church of St. Anne and relatively small-scale seventeenth and eighteenth century stone buildings".

Although it has never struck me before, I must concede that the Market Place really is funnel-shaped. It occurs to me that my shop is funnel-shaped too.

Bernard Lynam's *An Australian's Royal Britain* has the following entry for the Peak District: "Some of the main towns in the area are: Rudyard, Leek, Flash and Buxton".

Readers from Flash and Rudyard are likely to be flattered, and not a little surprised, by the inclusion of their small hamlets in this list. Readers from Bakewell and Matlock are likely to be somewhat offended by the omission of their towns!

A 1935 copy of S. P. B. Mais' *Round About England* contains a rather damning description of Buxton's entertainment offerings. Mais says that Buxton is, "by no stretch of the imagination, a gay town". He describes hazardous and adventurous journeys in a bath chair down steep gardens known as the Slopes, but says, "for the rest there seems only the choice between bowls, croquet and watching the ducks".

Mais would be even more dismissive of Buxton's attractions today - bowls, croquet and bath chairs have all disappeared from the spa area. 'Watching the ducks', however, is still available.

In Margaret Baker's *Folklore and Customs of Rural England* I could find no mention of the ancient Derbyshire custom of well-dressing. An amazing omission!

I spotted an advertisement for Manchester Airport on the back cover of one of my books. The promotion suggests that visitors to this country should fly into Manchester to "discover the real Britain. Scotland and Wales, the Lake District, the Yorkshire Dales, Chester, Viking York, Shakespeare's Stratford are all within easy reach of Britain's best airport".

No mention whatsoever of the Peak District which is right on Manchester's doorstep!

Michael Watkin's 1981 book *The English* has a chapter about Mary Bryant, the village schoolmistress at Flagg, near Buxton. A nature class trip to a pond is described in the book. Mary had sixteen children in her class. On the day of the pond visit, six were absent due to hay-making.

Here's England is "a Valentine for the most beautiful, wonderful, exciting country in Europe". It was written in the early fifties by two Americans, Ruth McKenney and Richard Bransten.

When Richard and Ruth came to England they fell in love with London, Oxford, Cambridge and the South-west. Most of their book is devoted to these areas, but they "thought the Lake District dull" - "Why spend a fortune crossing the Atlantic, and wind up by a waterfall eleven feet high?" ("The trip up to the saddle of the Jungrau is Scenery").

The Peak District fairs only marginally better than the Lake District:

"The Peak District, near Derby, has moderately good scenery".

Buxton is described as "a spa in the hills above Rowsley".

This week's whole-page newspaper advertisement for Buxton Spa Water features the baptism of a child by Father Higgins at St. Anne's Church. Father Higgins is said to be marvelling, "not for the first time", at "a Buxton baby's tendency to gurgle rather than cry".

According to the advertisement, the gurgling of Buxton babies could be caused by the consumption of the town's spa water which gurgles up through the Peak District limestone.

The local hoteliers must be gurgling too at the prospect of the flood of visitors which will spring from this advertisement!

Today I acquired a copy of *The Threat to the Peak*, published in 1932 by the C.P.R.E. The book, which identifies various eyesores on the fair face of the Peak, includes a particularly vitriolic attack on the design of petrol filling stations, with their crude advertising boards and their collections of "disorderly, garishly coloured shacks".

Heaven knows what the authors of this report would have made of current-day petrol stations with their vast illuminated canopies. On this very day I received a letter from Bryan McGee, who had seen a report in the local paper about my efforts as a Parish Councillor to promote an "Operation Facelift" in Chapel-en-le-Frith. In his letter Bryan describes the giant Esso garage in Chapel as "a monstrosity from the Mid-West of the U.S.A. which has been transposed to the heart of a Peak District town".

The British Selection, Arthur Eperon's 1985 guide to the best British hotels, includes a recommendation for the Cavendish Hotel at Baslow, a hotel which was renovated and then leased by the Duchess of Devonshire.

Eperon likes the Cavendish because it is possible to look out from the hotel across the Chatsworth Estate and "dream that you are a Duchess".

Ashley Courtney's 1953 edition of *Let's Halt Awhile in Britain and Ireland* has the following entry for the Isaac Walton Hotel at Dovedale:

"The pity of it is that so many motorists passing up and down the Ashbourne road are in too much of a hurry to turn off but three miles and relax amidst the green enfolding hills".

Today, the pity is that so many *do* turn off for Dovedale. On any Bank Holiday the green enfolding hills become one giant car park.

The *1976 CAMRA Good Beer Guide* contains the following entry for the Bull's Head at Ashford in the Water:

"Cows occasionally welcome".

Apparently, this is a reference to an occasion when the locals carried on drinking despite the intrusion of a cow which had wandered into the bar!

Humphrey Pakington's *English Villages and Hamlets* only features three Derbyshire villages: Alsop-en-le-dale, Parwich and Sparrowpit. Surprisingly, there is no mention of the "show villages" of Tissington, Castleton or Ashford-in-the-Water!

Sparrowpit is one of my own favourite hamlets. Its single street runs along a very high, exposed limestone ridge. Almost all the houses are on one side of the street. There are no numbers on the cottages; every house carries a name.

Pakington gives a nice description of the place: "a mere handful of grey houses and which yet has a certain picturesqueness as it stands stolidly facing the winds of heaven".

The *1951 Sunday Times Travel and Holiday Guide to Great*

Britain and Ireland has chapters devoted to Devon, Cornwall, Oxford, Cambridge, Stratford, Yorkshire, Lancashire, Wales, the Lakes and Scotland.

The Peak District does not feature in the guide at all and Derbyshire only gets a mention in the pages which list country houses which are open to the public!

I pinned up on my cuttings board the latest in the series of clever, full-page newspaper advertisements for Buxton Spring Water. This particular advertisement features a story about "Britain's Highest Barmaid" and a photograph of a young woman on a trampoline outside the Cat and Fiddle Inn, near Buxton.

The Cat and Fiddle is Britain's second highest pub (Tan Hill, in Yorkshire, being the highest) but, with the help of her trampoline, the bouncing barmaid in the photograph is able to achieve an altitude greater than that of Tan Hill!

I was delighted to find that Egon Ronay's *Pubs and Tourist Sights in Britain 1973* lists Chapel-en-le-Frith as a Peak District town "not to be missed".

Unfortunately, it is very easy to miss the attractions of the old Capital of the Peak, because the picturesque Old Town is largely hidden from view behind a very drab main street.

I have just written a paper for the parish council about the need to facelift Chapel. The paper is entitled *Chapel-en-le-Frith - The Peak District's Best Kept Secret or Its Most Neglected Asset.*

The *National Trust Guide to Follies*, by Headley and Meulenkamp, contains just one entry for my home town of Chapel-en-le-Frith. On a narrow road below Eccles Pike the authors came across a crenellated gateway which had been converted into a "picturesque sham" when a lorry crashed into it. Headley and Meulenkamp describe the structure as a "folly in the making".

Tony, one of my regular customers, told me about his American pen-friend, Charley Eckhardt:

Charley, who was raised on a Texas ranch, writes short stories about the American West. Two of his stories, *131 Blue Jay Road* and *Beef for Uncle Sam's Injuns*, have reached the finals of the Western Writers' Spur Award. Charley has also tried his hand at a detective novel which is based around events at a writers' convention at a fictitious country house near Chapel-en-le-Frith. Charley has never visited England, but has gathered his information about the Peak District from the letters which he has received from Tony.

Tony kindly lent me copies of magazines containing Charley's two short stories and he also asked if I would like to read and make comments on the manuscript of the Chapel-en-le-Frith detective novel. I loved the story *131 Blue Jay Road* and I wrote a critique of the detective novel, which Tony then sent on to Charley.

Later Tony brought me a copy of Charley's response to my critique. The following extract from his letter provides a good illustration of Charley's writing style:

"There's actually very little autobiographical material in the story. The central character is, of course, a composite, and there's a little of me, a little of my cousin Mike Lane (he's got what we call in Texas "panhandle teeth" - the lucky sucker grew up in Lubbock where the water is naturally heavily fluoridated and he's got teeth like granite, never had a cavity in his life, has never had to go to a dentist), a little of a pal of mine who was an infantry NCO in Nam (I was an artillery second lieutenant), a little of my friend John Tolleson, whose dad was an oil man who died very suddenly of a heart attack, and who - unfortunately for John - went broke one more time than he got rich; you get the picture".

Charley's letter is headed, "More Bombs and Poison from Charley", and ends:

"Keep yer tail over the dashboard ....

Charley".

Part of the Peak District collection.

Reflections

When I was a headteacher I had precious little time to pause and reflect.

Bookselling is a more leisurely occupation. There is even time to read the newspaper, to browse amongst the shelves, to stare out of the window, to simply let the mind wander. The subconscious mind often throws up novel connections when it is allowed to wallow in unhurried and unrestrained reflection.

A Life of leisure!? Mike now has time to sit and read the papers.

According to Jonathon Raban's new book *Bad Lands*, Ismay, Montana was re-named Joe, Montana as a tribute to Joe Montana, the American Football player. I spent a few idle moments musing over some place-name possibilities in this country:

Leonard, Cheshire
General, Westmoreland
Austin, Somerset
Susan, Hampshire
David, Essex
Bruce, Kent

Then I began to wonder if the county of Kent had ever declared itself a Nuclear Free Zone. Most unlikely!

Biographies which rubbish the recently-dead are highly fashionable at the moment and provide lucrative pickings for their unscrupulous authors.

Thomas Hardy had the answer. Some years after Hardy's death, his widow produced a very flattering biography of her husband. It later materialised that Hardy had written the book himself!

A customer asked me to find her a book of paintings by Beryl Cook.

Julian Spalding, the Director of Glasgow's new Museum of Modern Art, is currently under fire from critics for giving wall space to a

Beryl Cook painting - "Maybe the only modern art museum in the world to give a prominent place to the works of Beryl Cook".

Why do these same commentators consider it praiseworthy for the Director of the Tate Gallery to devote a whole wall to one of Roy Lichtenstein's highly-enlarged comic strip images?

Husband and wife journalists, Sean French and Nicci Gerard, have produced a jointly-written novel under the single nom-de-plume, Nicci French. Just imagine the pseudonyms and titles which could emerge from other collaborations:

Edna Barnes - *The Parrot with Green Eyes*
Shelagh Winterson - *A Taste of Oranges*
Joanna Fowles - *The French Lieutenant's Wife*
Anita Keillor - *Hotel du Lac Wobegon*
Clive Amis - *Unreliable Information*
Nicholas Updike - *The Rabbit Whisperer*
Muriel Hoeg - *Miss Brodie's Feeling for Snow*

etc., etc., etc.

When one of my customers spotted a still from an old Doris Day and Rock Hudson film in an old *Film Review*, she said, "Those films were wonderful. Doris Day would spend the entire film preserving her virginity. Nowadays, films are all full-frontal bonking". This remark brought to mind my first under-age visit (at the age of fifteen) to an X-certificate film. The most daring moment in the film, *The Seven-year Itch*, was a fleeting glimpse of Marilyn Monroe's knickers as her skirt was blown up by an air-vent. This week Jo-Ann and I went to the cinema for the first time in years. The film which we saw, *Stealing Beauty*, contained drug-taking, nudity, public urinating, and a lengthy sequence in which the young heroine loses her virginity. The film merely merits a 15-certificate!

Juxtaposing books on the display tables in the shop can be great fun. A few contrived juxtapositions:

The Downing Street Years, by Margaret Thatcher, next to
The View from No. 11 by Nigel Lawson.

Superwoman, by Shirley Conran, next to
Total Man, by Stan Gooch.

Books about the Royals provide some lovely juxtapositions:

The Spencers of Althorp, by Georgina Battiscombe, next to
The Royal House of Windsor, by Elizabeth Longford.

Royal Love Stories, by Margaret Nicholas, next to
Diana: A Princess and her Troubled Marriage, by Nicholas Davies.

Diana: Her True Story, by Andrew Morton, next to
Captain's Diary, by Will Carling.

I acquired some Dick Francis' first editions today. Some of the titles, such as *Whip Hand* and *Driving Force*, disturb me.

Last Christmas, when I learned that Adrian Maguire had won the King George VI Chase on Barton Bank after striking his horse ten times with the whip, I wrote to the letters page of the *Guardian*. In my letter I pointed out that the Jockey Club's Whip Rules offer little protection for horses in big races. Safe in the knowledge that a whipping offence does not carry a disqualification penalty, many jockeys are willing to risk a short suspension when driving their horses to the finishing post in the more prestigious races.

When we first opened the business, I had two publicity shots taken for the local paper. For one photograph, I posed in front of the shop; for the other picture, I posed inside the shop with a large illustrated biography of Augustus John in my hands. This morning I sold the John biography to a customer who reminded me of two lovely stories about Augustus:

The artist was a notorious womaniser and he fathered a great many children. It is said that he was in the habit of patting the heads of all the children in his locality just in case they happened to be his own offspring!

Augustus was also a shrewd judge of artistic merit. He once said: "Fifty years after my death I shall be remembered as Gwen John's brother".

Today I sold a large book of Lucian Freud portraits.

Freud has had many relationships with women, including many of his models, and he has fathered a great number of children - he is rumoured to have sired up to forty offspring, but acknowledges only seven - yet he paints human flesh as though it were raw meat and makes no attempt to flatter his subjects, whether they be female models or homosexual males.

One of his more unlikely sitters is the present Duke of Devonshire, from Chatsworth House. The Duke is reported to have said that he is grateful that it was he who was Freud's sitter rather than his daughter!

I have obtained a little book about the American artist, Edward Hopper. The book has a nice description of Hopper's subject matter - the artist loved to paint "houses which cast positive shadows".

I discovered the other day that Hopper's painting *House by the Railroad* was the inspiration for Bates' house in the film *Psycho*.

Douglas Gordon has just received this year's Turner Prize. One of his best known works is *24 hour Psycho*, a slowed down version of Hitchock's film which runs for twenty-four hours. The shower scene takes half-an-hour in Gordon's version!

The Joys of
Being an Author

Jill Dick is a Chapel-en-le-Frith based journalist who writes guidebooks for aspiring writers. In her book *Writing for Magazines* she describes the joy of being an author:

"I've never forgotten sitting in an aeroplane beside a party of young girls clutching copies of a particular magazine just bought in the airport bookshop. The cover told me to watch carefully as they turned the pages - yes! - to an article they pored over before starting an animated discussion about it. You've guessed, of course. They never knew the writer of the piece was sitting a few seats away as they read it and, I'm glad to say, praised it.

Sample the exhilaration and I promise that even when you're an old hand at writing for magazines, with countless published articles to your credit, it never diminishes".

I cannot claim to have seen young girls, or anyone else for that matter, reading one of my articles on an aeroplane, nor can I claim to be an old hand at writing, but I have experienced the thrill of watching a customer pick up and purchase one of my books in the local W. H. Smith's, and I must also confess to repeatedly caressing the covers of my first book when it finally appeared in print.

I went into a bookshop yesterday and experienced the rare pleasure of seeing one of my own publications on display. I picked up the book, pretended to consider a purchase, and then placed the copy in a more prominent spot on the shelves.

One advantage of owning my own shop is that I am able to give my own publications a position on the shelves which they deserve!!!

Mike's book on Chapel-en-le-Frith occupying the prominent position which it deserves !!!

A customer who asked me for books by Anthony Burgess reminded me of the story about Burgess' sacking from his job on the *Guardian*. Burgess was dismissed from the paper after he had written a review for the *Guardian* of one of his own books (which he had written under a nom-de-plume).

It strikes me that this method of reviewing has much to recommend it. Reviewers often betray a rather sketchy knowledge of the books which they seek to judge. At least Burgess could not be criticized for having an inadequate grasp of his subject!

After the publication of my first book (a little Peak District guidebook) I was appalled to read a review which contained the following passage: "The author describes Eyam and its infamous seventeenth century plague and points out the village's new plague - commercialism, the result of too many visitors".

My chapter on Eyam actually contained the following sentence: "Despite an enormous influx of visitors, Eyam has remained remarkably resistant to commercialisation".

The African American author, Terry McMillan, is due in Manchester tonight to give a reading at Waterstone's Deansgate store. Terry's last book sold 4 million copies, and 2,000 people turned up to one of her readings in an American bookstore. I recall that my one and only performance at a literary event (at a Peak District primary school) attracted just a dozen people, three of whom were relatives!

Jilly Cooper has said, "You get the ultimate orgasm getting your first book published". Most first-time authors would probably agree with this claim, but they would also report that satisfaction is rarely immediate. There is often a long delay between the acceptance of a first book and its appearance in print - I had to wait three years from the completion of my first manuscript to publication date. A long time coming!

An article which I wrote for the magazine *Modern Painters* has been included in this month's issue. The list of contributors contains the following entry:

"Mike Smith retired recently from the headship of Silverdale School. He now runs a bookshop in the Peak District".

A former teaching colleague who had seen the article rang to say how nice it must be to have the time in retirement to write pieces for magazines.

In fact, I wrote the article some months before my retirement. A long delay between manuscript submission and publication is a common experience for authors, at least for us lesser mortals!

Oliver asked me to search for a copy of Rowland Parker's *The Common Stream*, which he describes as the best book which he has read on local history.

Rowland Parker taught in the same school for thirty-seven years and spent thirteen years researching his book on the history of Foxton. This shining example of stickability rather puts in the shade my own efforts: I spent seventeen years teaching at Silverdale School and just three months researching my book *Chapel-en-le-Frith in Old Picture Postcards*.

I was asked to find a batch of *Conan* books by Robert E. Howard.

The use of the middle initial, once much favoured by U.S. presidents, has rather gone out of fashion these days, save for its use by a few authors.

My very first article for a magazine, *The New Scientist*, was captioned:

"by Michael J. Smith, who teaches Chemistry at Dinnington High School."

I was feeling rather pleased with my first appearance in print until a friend brought me down to earth by suggesting the caption should have read:

"Michael J. Smith of Dinnington H. School."

Poor Robert Noonan. The manuscript for his one-and-only book, *The Ragged Trousered Philanthropists* was rejected by several publishers during his lifetime and only published after his death. Even then, it was published under the pen-name Robert Tressell.

I had always wanted my name to appear on the spine of a book. When this finally came about I was disappointed to find that my publishers had printed the spine with the head of the letters towards the rear cover, rather than towards the front cover. I can only find a handful of books in my shop with this spine arrangement - some Penguins from the forties, some old books from the *Britain in Pictures* series, a couple of Dent hardbacks from the forties and a 1951 *Sunday Times Travel Guide*.

As a result of its quirky spine arrangement, my own little book already looks like a long-forgotten paperback from the forties!

I bought some science text books today. Amongst them was a copy of Liptrot's *Modern Inorganic Chemistry*. At the end of Chapter Four there is a list of suggested reading. The references include the following entry:

M. J. Smith *Ionisation Potentials, Periodicity and Electronic Configuration*, School Science Review, No. 170, Vol 49, 1968.

Another ambition satisfied. I have always wanted to be quoted as a reference and, at long last, I have found what is probably the one and only text book reference to one of my scientific papers.

Today's *Guardian* contains a double page spread about the reaction of artists and writers to beastly reviews of their works.

The article, by Michael Billington, was prompted by Kitaj's painting *The Critic Kills*. Kitaj believes that his wife's death was brought on by the vicious reviews which accompanied his 1994 retrospective exhibition at the Tate. The painting is the artist's response to his critics.

The same issue of the *Guardian* contains a critical review by Natasha Walter of Penelope Lively's new novel *Heat Wave*. The piece opens with "Is Penelope Lively capable of writing an interesting sentence?" and closes with "Lively has a way of turning all she touches to lead".

Billington believes that wounded artists and writers should maintain a stoical silence. I wonder if Penelope Lively is feeling stoical today?

Jilly Cooper is reported as saying, "Forty per cent of the books published in this country are rubbish". Does she include her own books in this category?

A couple of tourists asked if I had any copies of *The Look Again Guide to the Peak*. They told me that they had read the book in their hotel room and enjoyed its descriptions of Peak District towns and villages. Delighted by this unexpected comment, I readily owned up to being the author. I then had to explain that copies are no longer available - the little guidebook suffered a remaindered death some years ago.

I felt like a dead author, unrecognised in his lifetime, who has suddenly achieved a little posthumous recognition.

Authors often take extraordinary steps to minimise distractions when they are writing. According to an article in today's paper, Somerset Maugham once asked a builder to block up a window in his roof-top study at La Mauresque, on the French Riviera. The window provided a panoramic view of the Baie des Anges. The builder, who could not bring himself to carry out the permanent obliteration of this vista suggested Maugham cover the window with a large painting.

Rather incongruously, the newspaper article is accompanied by a photograph of Maugham, in dressing gown and slippers, standing at an open window and looking out over the Baie des Anges. I cut out the picture and stuck it to my pin-board as a reminder of a particularly memorable view of the Mediterranean which Jo-Ann and I once enjoyed from an open window in the Picasso Museum at Antibes.

The window in my own roof-top study in Chapel-en-le-Frith has a superb view of Combs Moss, a high gritstone ridge with a Table Mountain-like profile. The window is above head-height, but there is a small ladder which provides viewing access. The ladder is a sign of my weakness - I am all too willing to be distracted from my work by this wonderful Peak District panorama.

Authors as Celebrities

Actor turned novelist, Hugh Laurie, has said that his fantasy would be to live and write in the Outer Hebrides and simply post off his finished books to his publisher. He claims to hate the "modern nonsense" of promotion, press reaction, reviews, literary evenings and signing sessions. Hugh claims that the process of promotion is "completely at odds with the solitary business of writing and reading",

How many other authors share this negative view of book promotion is open to question. Jo-Ann and I attend a good number of literary evenings, and we have formed the impression that most authors enjoy these evenings just as much as their readers do. Cynics would argue that the prospect of boosting sales, and hence royalties, is enough to put a smile on the face of any author, but most writers seem to welcome a chance to meet their readers face-to-face, and almost all of them read from their own work with some degree of passion and with a great deal of pride.

Jo-Ann and I attended a party at Waterstone's for the launch of *Bloomsbury Quids,* little editions of short stories to celebrate Bloomsbury's first decade as a publishing house. Two of the speakers were Will Self and Candia McWilliam.

In the photographs used to caption Will Self's newspaper columns, the author looks like a cross between Dracula and Norman Tebbitt. In the flesh he is a very affable and attractive young man. Jo-Ann was quite taken with him.

Candia McWilliam`s appearance was even more surprising. I bought my first Candia McWilliam book purely on the strength of the photograph of the author on the back cover. The picture depicts a dark-haired sensuous beauty. When Candia walked into Waterstone's I was taken by surprise. The author is indeed attractive but her face is topped by a rather unruly mop of blond hair. Her dress sense is equally surprising - I had expected her to be wearing some slinky black dress, but she turned up in a loose-fitting, white sari.

However, when Candia signed my copy of her book and expressed pleasure at meeting someone as tall as herself, I was completely charmed by her.

Beryl Bainbridge's latest novel is based on events surrounding the sinking of the Titanic. I discovered from today`s newspaper that Beryl has also produced some very large, gloomy paintings to represent the tragic event. When I heard that Beryl had a new novel out I felt quite buoyant. When I heard that she had also become an artist I got a sinking feeling!

I obtained a cut price copy of Alan Bennett`s *Writing Home*. The book sold within one hour of its being placed in the window.

A couple of years ago, Jo-Ann and I attended a Waterstone`s literary evening for the launch of the book.

Bennett is a wonderful humorist: he has the knack of poking fun at people in a way which is totally inoffensive. During his on-stage performance at the literary event, he even got away with making a joke about his own mother`s senile dementia.

Alan Bennett and I both developed our love of reading at Armley Library in Leeds - but against all odds! During the signing session, Alan told me that he had found Armley`s Junior Library (which was in the basement of the library building and was presided over by a fierce British Legion commissionaire) a most depressing place. I told him that I had equally unpleasant memories of the children`s section. I used to visit the library every Friday night with my father and he used to smuggle me upstairs into the much brighter, more welcoming adult library.

Last night`s television programme in the *Secret Lives* series gave a portrait of Enid Blyton far removed from her popular image. There was even a suggestion that Ms Blyton may have locked her children in a cupboard when she did not wish to be disturbed during writing sessions. In my youthful innocence I had pictured the author as the prototype for Aunt Fanny in the *Famous Five* series. Although she is the long-suffering wife of the obsessive, bad-tempered Uncle Quentin, Aunt Fanny is a kindly and tolerant character. My illusions are shattered - it would now seem that Enid Blyton is actually the prototype for grumpy Uncle Quentin!

The programme also contained a claim that Ms Blyton was in the habit of playing strip tennis. You cannot be serious!!

It is said that people write books in order to achieve some form of immortality. As the following letter demonstrates, some authors hedge their bets by staking their claim to more than one after-life:

"Dear Mr Smith,

Please find enclosed my 'wants list' of books. I have enclosed a £3.00 search fee as there are three different authors on my list, albeit they are the same person -

James Hadley Chase
Raymond Marshall
James L Docherty"

Jo-Ann and I went to the Colin Thubron literary evening in Manchester.

Mr Thubron came across as a thoughtful, attractive, but lonely man. He alternates travel-writing with novel-writing; long periods alone in faraway places are punctuated by shorter periods of isolation in a remote cottage where he writes his fiction.

I asked the author if he would like to be remembered for his travel-writing or for his novels. He said he would much prefer to be remembered for the novels, because "it is much harder to write fiction than descriptive travel pieces".

I was surprised to hear of his admiration for the late Bruce Chatwin. Their styles of travel-writing are so very different: Chatwin seeks out the obscure, the fantastic and the bizarre; Thubron simply describes what he sees - but so poetically!

I rang a Manchester bookshop to ask if Jeanette Winterson would be attending a literary evening to promote her new novel *Gut Symmetries*.

Assistant: "Ms Winterson does not do literary evenings".

Self: "Don't all publishers demand it of their authors these days?"

Assistant: "There are some authors whom publishers can't dictate to. She's one of them".

Self: "Has she ever done literary evenings at your shop?"

Assistant: "She hates them. She won't even come into the room if she sees a man in the audience who is wearing shorts". (a very odd comment to make on a January day!)

The assistant's remarks are a wonderful addition to the fund of (apocryphal?) stories about Winterson.

The Booker Prize season is here again. The prize has an enormous effect on book sales - when Anita Brookner's novel *Hotel du Lac* was first published it was given a print run of only 4,000 copies. By the end of 1984, after its success in the Booker Prize, the book had sold 50,000 copies!

Jo-Ann and I went to a Waterstone's literary evening to see Edna O'Brien.

Edna is stunningly attractive. She has a beautifully-lyrical voice and a warm smile. She is an intoxicating mix of modesty and haughtiness: when taking a question from the audience she is charming and deferential to her inquisitor, but when she articulates her response she holds her head up high and raises her hand in a grand theatrical gesture.

I asked her the following pre-prepared question:

"In your book *Mother Ireland* you say that leaving Ireland was "no wrench" and that Ireland filled you with fears. Have you revised your opinion about the wrench and do you still carry the fears?"

I was far too mesmerised by the beauty of Edna's voice and overcome by the fact that she was actually speaking to me, to catch the precise details of her answer, but I gathered that her affection for Ireland has increased over the years and that she admits to carrying fears "like all the rest of us".

Jo-Ann and I decided that we would go along to Waterstone's to see the African American author, Terry Macmillan, who has become a one-woman phenomenon. The bookshop was packed to the rafters, largely by young Afro-Caribbean women. Terry read her splendid stream-of-consciousness prose with tremendous fluency and passion. In the question-time which followed, the audience showed great good humour and also a total lack of inhibition. Terry faced close questioning about her private life, but she answered frankly and fully, and with a grace and sense of fun which matched that of her interrogators. The members of the audience displayed obvious delight in their heroine's hugely successful career as an author and also in her new-found happiness in her personal life. It is very evident that Terry represents the twin aspirations of so many young Afro-Caribbean women - a rewarding career and a fulfilling love-life.

Jo-Ann and I went to Manchester to see Clive James promote his new novel *Silver Castle*. It was a disappointing evening. James read from the book for far too long - about forty minutes - and he wasn't at all keen to take any questions from the floor which were not directly related to his new novel. His answers were rambling and even evasive. James does show obvious concern for the poor and underprivileged - hence his book, which is about a poor Indian boy who wanders into the world of "Bollywood" (Bombay cinema). However, the evening left us with the impression that Clive James has a much greater concern - his concern for Clive James!

If the truth be known, I became disillusioned with Clive James many years ago. His television crits in the Observer were once the high point of my Sunday mornings - until I read a piece by James which dismissed animal rights protesters as sentimental old fools. The final straw came when I watched James' sycophantic T.V. interview with Ronald Reagan in which he allowed the ex-President to get away with ludicrous claims that he had restored Democracy to Central America.

I still have copies of an *Interview Advice* sheet which I used to give out to my sixth formers. One of the bullet points on the sheet is:

"Always keep your hands away from your face during a selection interview".

It would seem that writers receive very different advice when they pose for publicity photographs. I found the following mug shots in recent publishers' magazines:

Alan Bennett - bespectacled eyes framed by his hands which are spread out across his cheeks. (Presumably this pose is designed to portray the "Whimsical Observer". In fact, Alan looks as if he's expressing alarm at having accidentally knocked over an expensive vase).

Melvyn Bragg - one bent finger resting lightly on his chin. (Presumably, this pose is designed as the sexy gesture of the "Thinking Woman's Crumpet". In fact, Melvyn looks as if he's picking a nasty spot on his chin)

Ben Elton - one extended finger resting on his temple. (Presumably, this pose is designed to portray the "Quick-fire Thinker". In fact, Ben appears to be suffering from a piercing headache over one eye).

David Baddiel - stubbly chin resting on his fist. (Presumably, this pose is designed to represent a "Nineties' Lad". In this case, the depiction is entirely accurate: David looks as if he's having great difficulty propping up a head which is suffering from a massive hang-over - the result of very 'laddish' behaviour!)

Mike's sketches of David Baddiel and Alan Bennett.

Celebrities as Authors

Carmen Callil, chair of this year's Booker judges, is quoted as saying, "only novelists should write books". Maybe this explains the omission from the 1997 Booker short-list of Ben Elton's *Popcorn*, which had been strongly tipped for inclusion by some commentators.

Stephen Fry, Eleanor Bron, Ned Sherrin, Hugh Laurie, Jane Asher, Michael Palin and David Baddiel have all taken to novel-writing in recent times. Perhaps there should now be a "Literary Luvvie Award" for the Best Actor Turned Novelist!

The latest celebrity to try her hand at novel-writing is actress and cake-maker Jane Asher. According to this month's *Books Magazine*, Jane was encouraged to write a novel by a publisher who had read in a newspaper interview that Jane's literary preferences included Martin Amis, A. S. Byatt and early Iris Murdoch.

I like Jane's selection of authors - Amis' *Visiting Mrs Nabokov* is the very best collection of modern journalism I have read, Murdoch's *Unofficial Rose* is the book which first got me hooked on modern literary fiction, and I take out and read over and over again my copy of A. S. Byatt's wonderful description of her first visit to Provence.

Do these literary preferences qualify me to write a novel too, or must I learn to act and make cakes before I receive the call from a publisher?

News is just out that Bob Dylan has been nominated for the Nobel Prize for Literature. Should I move my copy of Dylan's one and only novel *Tarantula* to the literary criticism shelves?

Ben Elton's latest novel *Popcorn* is being tipped for the Booker Prize short-list. Should I move my copy of *Stark* from the popular fiction shelves to join Bob Dylan's *Tarantula* in the literary fiction section?

Humour was much in evidence at two Manchester literary evenings which featured members of the Monty Python team. When Michael Palin and Terry Jones came along to promote their books, they both decided to stray from their brief.

Michael Palin began an evening which had been billed as a promotion for *Hemingway's Chair* by reading side-splitting quotes from one of his schoolboy essays.

When Terry Jones came along to promote his *Book of Pressed Fairies* he entered into an hilarious collusion with his audience by discussing his book as if it were an historically important, factually-accurate account of fairy sightings. When he grew bored with this pretence he pulled out of his briefcase a pre-publication copy of *Crusades* and began to promote his television series about the Crusades. But the evening ended with Terry selling lots of *Pressed Fairy* books to his fans.

One young man had a particularly memorable evening. Before collecting his signed copy from Terry he handed his camera to a lady in the queue and asked her if she would take a commemorative picture for him. In preparation for the pose, he took off his anorak, removed his spectacles, combed his hair, and placed his arm on the comedian's shoulder.

The young man will now be able to boast to his friends that he has actually met and held a conversation with Terry Jones, and he will have a photograph to prove it!

Cutting Remarks

The pin-board next to my serving desk contains some essential information - notes from customers, business cards of booksellers, publishers and distributors, essential telephone numbers - but most of the contents of the board are items selected for my own pleasure and amusement during long days in the shop - art cards acquired at recently-visited art exhibitions, photographs taken on family holidays, postcards sent to me by customers, clippings from newspapers.

Cuttings board in High Street Bookshop.

Newspaper cuttings and art cards are also on display around the shop, to give customers some light amusement during the serious business of browsing.

On my pin-board I keep a lovely picture of the novelist Iris Murdoch and her philosopher husband John Bayley.

The photographer has captured them at their kitchen table. Iris' hair is lank and uncombed; she is wearing what appears to be a pinny. John is wearing a flat-cap and an open-necked shirt; he appears to have forgotten to put his teeth in. On the table there is a half-eaten biscuit and a jar of coffee-mate.

A customer who spotted the picture asked if it was a photograph of my parents. I didn't know whether to feel flattered or insulted!

A lady asked me if I would display a small poster for a concert to be given at the Palace Hotel by young local cellist, Amy Langley. The photograph on the poster shows Amy embracing her cello whilst looking up at the camera with, what my mother would call, come-to-bed eyes. I am sure that the concert will be a sell-out!

Books about the art of Edward Hopper are very popular.

On my wall I keep a cutting from the *Guardian* of Peter Doig's description of Hopper's *Summer Evening*, a painting which depicts a couple in the porch of a weather-boarded house in the late evening of a summer's day.

When Doig looks at this evocative painting for a long time he "starts to hear the deafening sound of crickets".

A customer noticed some photographs of Catalonia on my personal pin-board. He told me that both his grandparents had come from Catalonia - his mother from Roussillon and his father from Barcelona. After their marriage they had moved to Paris and some years later they settled in Lisbon. This all sounded very romantic until he told me that they had then moved to Scunthorpe!

I cut out a wonderful phrase from this morning's *Independent* and then placed the cutting by the Art shelves. Commenting on the De Kooning Retrospective, Andrew Graham-Dixon said: "De Kooning's genius is inseparable from his essential indecency".

Critics often write vicious reviews of books by well-established authors, but they seem to reserve their most venomous attacks for criticism of books which have been written by other critics.

Today's *Guardian* carries a review by Nicholas Lezard of A. A. Gill's novel *Sap Rising*. Gill is a critic on the *Sunday Times*. The review is headed, "Do not buy this book" and the piece ends with the suggestion that Gill is a "wanker".

Book reviewers can be unbelievably cruel. Carmen Callil says in her review of Olivia Goldsmith's *Bestseller*, "no cash should pass from reader to bookseller for this piece of work".

I placed the following quotation from J. G. Ballard on the Science Fiction shelves:

"The moon landing did not have the impact that it might have done, as we'd been there before. Science fiction had got there first".

A book by Arthur Marshall about schooldays contains a lovely quote from a school report:

"Johnny is so bad at Geography, I am surprised he finds his way home".

When I read this book I was reminded of a scribbled note which I once wrote at the end of a pupil's essay. The pupil pointed out to me that I had written:

"Please take more care with your speling". (sic)

The Degas Exhibition is drawing large crowds to a London gallery at the present time. I placed one of my books on Degas in the window, together with a press cutting which described Degas thus:

"A reactionary anti-semite, a misogynist, a half-blind photo-phobic hypochondriac and a curmudgeonly, misanthropic recluse".

Nice man!

I am always on the look out for picture postcards and newspaper cuttings for use as illustrations alongside the wording on my shelf direction signs. Some of the pictures currently in use are:

SOCIOLOGY >
(The direction sign to Sociology is illustrated by the classic photograph of John Cleese, Ronnie Barker and Ronnie Corbett representing the upper, middle and lower classes).

ART & PHOTOGRAPHY >
(Illustrated by Robert Capa's photograph of Picasso holding a beach umbrella above the head of Francoise Gillot).

SCIENCE >
(Illustrated by a picture of Stephen Hawking sitting in his constant technological companion - a wheelchair with attached voice

synthesizer).

TRANSPORT >

(Illustrated by a clever composite photograph of a 2CV in which ballet shoes have been substituted for wheels. The picture is captioned "Pas de Deux Chevaux").

INTERIOR DESIGN >

(Illustrated by a photograph, from *Modern Painters* magazine, which shows Terence Conran patting the bottom of a hermaphrodite figure on a mural by Allen Jones).

CRAFTS >

(Illustrated by a postcard, from the Louvre, of Vermeer's picture *The Lacemaker* - a delicately-painted picture of a delicate subject).

POLITICS >

(Illustrated by the famous newspaper photograph of Nelson Mandella and Betty Boothroyd holding hands as they walk down the steps at Westminster).

CLASSIC CRIME >

(Illustrated by a classic drawing, by Sidney Paget, from *Strand Magazine*. Holmes conducts a chemical experiment whilst Watson looks on in awe and admiration).

TRAVEL >

(Illustrated by a photograph of Robert and Sonia Delaunay and Arp travelling through the South of France in a large open-top touring car. Sonia, who occupies the back seat, is sheltering grandly from the sun under a parasol which matches a dress of her own design).

ANTIQUES >

(Illustrated by a wonderful photograph, by Tom Stuttard, of a pair of elderly male clock collectors. The two are pictured sitting side-by-side in bed below a wall which is completely covered by antique grandfather clocks. The picture carries the caption "Bedtime with a touch of English eccentricity").

SPORT >

(Illustrated by a photograph of a pensive Eric Cantona. The picture is captioned: "Eric Cantona dabbles in philosophy; Albert Camus was a goalie").

MUSIC AND DANCE >

(Illustrated by a postcard reproduction of Picasso's *Three Dancers* - a brilliant evocation, on a static and two dimensional canvas, of movement and music).

FILM >

(Illustrated by a photograph of the audience at a 3-D cinema show. As all the film goers are wearing identical 3-D spectacles, they look, at first glance, like a set of clones. However, this effect is counterbalanced by the great variety of facial expressions on view. It is a funny moment in the film and some members of the audience are almost hysterical with laughter, others merely smile, whilst a significant minority remain totally poker-faced).

In The Trade

Hay-on-Wye is the book-lover's idea of Heaven, a browser's paradise. The town contains no less than twenty-three second-hand bookshops!

Hay is the supreme example of the pulling power of a town which has a conglomeration of second-hand bookshops. Buxton cannot yet rival Hay, but our town does have six independent bookshops - sufficient to encourage bibliophiles to make a special visit. Last year the independent booksellers of Buxton clubbed together to produce a *Buxton for Books* pamphlet, in order to encourage visitors to make a Grand Tour of the town's bookshops. Judged on the number of customers who are to be seen clutching the pamphlet as they enter our premises, the promotion has been a success.

Second-hand bookshops benefit from the presence of other bookshops in town and also from cooperation between booksellers. When I am unable to locate a book for a customer, I often ring David Huxley, at Hall Bank Bookshop, to ask if he has a copy. David and I do not regard ourselves as rivals; we cooperate on many matters and frequently suggest to our customers that they should pay a visit to the other second-hand bookshop in town.

The world of second-hand bookdealers is also characterised by helpfulness, good manners and cooperation. Bookdealers abide by an unwritten code of honesty. They give accurate descriptions (blemishes and all) of the books which they have to offer and ensure a prompt postal delivery.

The second-hand book trade remains unblemished by the "unacceptable face of capitalism".

I pinned up a cutting from the *Daily Telegraph Colour Supplement's Social Stereotypes* series. This week's subject is *The Second-Hand Bookseller*.

The stereotypical second-hand bookseller is portrayed as an overweight character with a wardrobe culled from *Brideshead Revisited*; he has limited academic prowess, but has re-invented himself up as a cultural dilettante and harbours secret ambitions to be a best-selling author.

Ouch!

The new Borders Bookstore in Manhattan has become New York's new "in-place". Book-buying is only one of the many activities which take place in the shop. Customers call in to browse, drink coffee, relax and to carry out their research. One technical writer, who does half a day's research in the store at a stretch, explained his habit to Ian Katz:

"In a bookshop you don't have to deal with the underclass and homeless you find in libraries".

I am reminded of an article I once read about a second-hand bookshop in Paris. One customer would take a book off the shelves and then settle down for a good read in the armchair provided. Before replacing the book on the shelf, he would turn down the corner of a page, in order to mark his place in readiness for his next visit!

One dealer who offers me books in response to my national 'wants list' always attaches a detailed description of the books which he is able to offer. He must devote considerable time to the composition of these synopses. Take his description of Dalton's *Borne on the Wind*:

"1st Edition, 1975. Large Format, 12" by 9", 160 pages, well illustrated in colour and monochrome, jacket somewhat torn, slight tears around edges, else good. The pioneering work of Dalton, who built much of his own equipment as none was available commercially. An inspiration for all lovers of action macro-photography, one of the most difficult of all subjects for the camera, as the subject is tiny, highly unpredictable and moves itself and its wings at an incredible rate in relation to the body - - - needing ultra-fast camera shutters, powerful electronic flashes operating at 1/20,000 sec. or less, and special high-speed trigger mechanisms. Even so, many hundreds or thousands of exposures can be needed to take a technically perfect photo, never mind one that also displays great beauty, as do Dalton's".

There speaks a real enthusiast!

Our short half-term holiday break in Hexham turned into a busman's holiday when we visited Barter Books in Alnwick. The bookshop, which is housed in old railway station buildings, carries a claim that it is one of the largest second-hand bookshops in England. Coffee-making facilities, biscuits, a warm coal-fire and armchairs are all provided as an aid to leisurely browsing. Now if ever I am able to afford larger premises ....

Jo-Ann, Charlotte and I made a visit to the Hockney exhibition at Manchester City Art Gallery.

In the Sixties Hockney produced some refreshing and highly original works of art, but much of Hockney's recent work is highly derivative. Chairs are used to indicate absent people (Van Gogh), colour is vivid and unreal (Matisse) and cubist techniques are used to cheat conventional perspective (Picasso).

Visitors to the exhibition were invited to fax their own art work to the gallery for display on a "Fax Wall". After seeing Hockney's pastiches of Van Gogh, Matisse and Picasso, I decided to produce my own pastiche of Hockney's fax art.

Before leaving for work today I asked Jo-Ann if she would send my fax-art to Manchester City Art Gallery and also post a rare book to a customer. I left the fax and the book on a table in the living room. At 9.30 am Jo-Ann phoned to tell me that our new puppy had eaten a corner out of my work of art and chewed up the rare book. I felt that Hockney, who is a great dog lover, would appreciate the tooth-marked work of art. My customer would be less pleased with the news about his book!

Portrait of D.H. by M.J.S.   '96

One browser told me of a bookseller, a former scientist who had experienced a term of imprisonment during the war for refusing to work on projects with a military purpose. My customer also has a friend who was a conscientious objector and she decided that it would be appropriate for two men of like mind to meet. When she introduced her friend to the bookseller the meeting did not go well.

My customer's friend said to the bookseller, "I understand that you were a "conshie" in the war too".

The bookseller replied, "Certainly not. I was an anarchist!"

Today's *Guardian* reports the destruction of the fine book collection of Sir Frank Kermode, former Professor of English Literature at Cambridge. It seems that Sir Frank asked three dustmen, whom he mistook for removal men, to take away thirty boxes of books which contained his collection of first editions, priceless manuscripts and books with personal dedications. This is a tragic illustration of the principle which governs my second-hand book business:

"One person's rubbish is another person's treasure".

One customer told me that he had once bought a second-hand book business for his wife. Unfortunately, his wife had been forced to quit the shop after only a couple of years, as the dust from the books had exacerbated her asthmatic condition.

This story gives a whole new meaning to the term "dust-jacket"!

I called in at a major bookseller's yesterday to check up on the Penguin and Oxford editions of Swift's *Gulliver's Travels*. As I was unable to find a copy, I asked an assistant if she could help me locate the book.

"Have you looked in our Travel section?" she said!

The names and addresses of dealers and booksellers on the booksearch network evoke an England of old world villages, graceful Georgian towns and elegant watering places. Consider the following list of shops and dealers from whom I have obtained books in recent weeks:

Bookshops:

Cobweb Books, Castle Hill Books, Chapter House Books, Twiggers, Tall Storeys Bookshop, Eton Antique Bookshop, Yesterday's Books, Periwinkle Press, Wayfarer Books, Treasures, Leaf Ends, Armchair Books.

Cottage homes of dealers:

Yew Tree Cottage, Green Willows, Rose Cottage, Old School House, The Furlongs, Wool Hanger Manor, Fair Acre, Owls Hill, Anvil Cottage, Moon Cottage, Thistledome, The Grange, Woodside Cottage, The Pastures.

Home towns of dealers whom I picture as living in gentle and happy retirement in their book-lined bungalows by the sea:

Ryde, Brighton, Bournemouth, Hove, East Looe, Weston super Mare, Hastings, Porlock, Scarborough, Lyme Regis, Formby, Horsham.

A selection of English village names taken from the addresses of dealers:

Clifton Campville, Upton-on-Severn, Chandlers Ford, Midsomer Norton, Eaton Ford, Little Shelford, Castlemorton, Old Netley.

Country town locations:

Wisbech, Coggeshall, Malvern, Abingdon, Leamington Spa, Cheltenham, Canterbury, Clifton, Chester, Helston, Framlingham, Cambridge, Launceston, Exeter, Ludlow, Bradford on Avon.

Two antiquarian booksellers from Australia came in to buy books about South-east Asia and Japan. It seems that Asian visitors are to Australian bookshops what American visitors are to British bookshops.

Proof of the effectiveness of our *Buxton for Books* campaign came today. A bookdealer from Newcastle-under-Lyme told me that he had come book-hunting in Buxton this week as he did not have the time to travel down to Hay-on-Wye.

Books obtained from the *Bookdealer* search network are purchased from bookdealers on the evidence of written descriptions of the condition of books on offer. There is a very strict protocol about the use of descriptions such as "fine", "very good", "good", and "reading copy only". One dealer sent me a book and inserted the following note:

"I have discovered that the condition of the book is not "fine", as I reported to you. Please accept my apologies for an inaccurate description and please accept the book as a free gift.

Reply not. I wish you well. You will love the book and make a decent living to boot.

Kind regards..."

Books are Treasure Chests

When Terry Jones, of Monty Python fame, gave television viewers a tour of his personal book collection, he confessed that he has not actually read most of the books in his library. Terry uses his books as sources of information and inspiration; he loves dipping into them.

Dipping into second-hand books is like finding an old box of documents and artefacts in the attic. Second-hand books are treasure chests. Dip into them and you will find evocative inscriptions, tender dedications, telling phrases, revealing annotations, wonderful quotations, surprising index references, and all manner of inserts, from newspaper cuttings to pressed flowers.

One of the Georgette Heyer first editions which I acquired today contains the following written dedication:

"To two of the most charming people I have known".

My second-hand copy of James Gorman's *First Aid for Hypochondriacs* contains the following dedication:

"Happy 21st Birthday Bill. To remind you of your butch image at school!

from Smithy"

In a copy of Balzac's *The Wild Ass's Skin* I found a sheet of paper which contained a hand-written selection of epitaphs. One example:

"Beneath this slab
John Brown is stowed
He watched the ads
And not the road"

Today I acquired a 1973 copy of *Know Britain - The Heritage and Institutions of an Offshore Island*. Before shelving the book I flicked through its pages.

I learned from the section on politics that 35% of British prime ministers (up to 1973) had been educated at Eton. A passage from Anthony Sampson's *Changing Anatomy of Britain* came to mind. According to Sampson, the old charge against Etonians was that they were confident, stupid and out of touch with the lives and needs and most people in the country. The new charge against Old Etonians is that they are confident, clever - but still out of touch.

I found an intriguing postcard between the pages of a second-hand book about Anglo-Japanese politics. The message on the card began:

"Dearheart, I expect C. J. has filled you in by now on all the naughty bits."

James Lees-Milne's *Fourteen Friends*, which had been ordered by Oliver, arrived today. I noticed that the publishers have printed only one testimonial on the dust-jacket, and this is by the Duchess of Devonshire, from nearby Chatsworth House. The Duchess says of Lees-Milne's book: "It is so good - as if his friends had just walked into the room".

"Debo" Devonshire has a mention in Lees-Milne's chapter on John Fowler, a designer who insisted on the correct use of moulds, cyma erecta and cyma reversa, and a strict observance of Vitruvian orders. Debo nicknamed him "Simon Erecta".

In Roy Hattersley's book *A Yorkshire Boyhood* there is a lovely reference to George Beeley, who was the Senior Teacher on my staff at Silverdale School. George and Roy both attended Sheffield's City Grammar School. George is described by Roy as "a languid member of the First XI".

I discovered that my paperback copy of *Pushed in the Wings*, by the Australian writer, Ross Fitzgerald, has pages 97 to 112 printed upside-down.

A reminder that Mr Fitzgerald comes from "Down-under"?

Before leaving for a short break in Winchester I looked up the city in a copy of the *Oxford Illustrated Literary Guide*. I found a nice description by Keats: "The side streets here are excessively maiden-like".

This quotation came to mind when we called in for morning coffee at Winchester Cathedral's coffee shop. The shop is run by very refined, elderly lady members of the National Trust.

This morning I found a cutting from the *Times* between the pages of an old copy of Hugh Brogan's *Life of Arthur Ransome*.

The newspaper article, entitled *Swallows and Bolsheviks*, and dated 31st December 1994, is by Professor Christopher Andrews. The professor claims that Ransome was seen by Cheka (the forerunner of the KGB) as their most important intelligence source on British foreign policy.

Brogan is rather less direct in his accusations - he does not name Ransome as an intelligence agent, but he does suggest that many of Ransome's newspaper pieces amounted to little more than Communist propaganda.

It seems to me that these attempts to discredit Ransome are rather unfair. The author made no secret of his political sympathies and his second wife was Trotsky's secretary. Does this necessarily mean he was an agent working to undermine the British state?

This afternoon I received by post a copy of Arthur Ransome's *Pigeon Post*. Inside the book I found a label with the inscription:

New College School, Oxford
History and Geography Prize
to
John Howitt Wilson
Form III 1944-45

No doubt some learned professor will write an article suggesting that a top Oxford school was a training ground for KGB agents.

I read Hunter Davies' biography of A. N. Wainwright whilst I was in the shop today. I was interested to read that Wainwright used the Palace Hotel, Buxton, as a base during the researching of his book on the Pennine Way.

I was even more interested to read of crusty old A.N.W.'s life-long lust for Betty Ditchfield.

Uffa Fox tells a nice story in his introduction to the *Fourteenth Giles Annual*:

During the last war, a shopkeeper, whose shop had just been battered by bombs, put a notice in the front of his premises (without doors or windows) which read: "OPEN AS USUAL". A few doors away there was another shop which had been blown wide open in the bombing. It carried the notice: "MORE OPEN THAN USUAL".

My own shop has been under siege throughout the week. Roadworks, designed to secure the future of Buxton's pelican crossing into the next Millennium, are taking place right outside my door. Persistent pneumatic drilling is hardly conducive to book-browsing or telephone conversations with publishers!

Today I obtained a 1966 copy of a Tate Gallery publication, *British Painting since 1945*. The book contains a reproduction of *Still Life with a Chip Frier*, by John Bratby. Obviously a work of art from the 'Kitchen Sink' genre of the Fifties. But was the theme always interpreted quite so literally?!

Even the *Literary Review* contains spelling mistakes. January's issue contains the following classified ad.:

"Postgraduate couple with child seek self-contained accomodation". (sic).

A batch of books which I bought today includes a large-format, beautifully-illustrated book called *The World of Flags*, by William Crampton. I was pleased to find the book in excellent condition, but when I flicked through the pages I noticed just one blemish - the illustration of the national flag of China had been cut-out and removed.

Was this one reader's method of making a personal protest against the Tiananmen Square Massacre?

I found a touching dedication in a second-hand paperback biography of Mahler:

"Thank you for a second chance, darling.
love Anna".

The fact that the book has now found it's way into my shop suggests that Anna did not get a third chance!

Before leaving for our summer break in Catalonia, I had searched the shelves for information on the architecture and culture of Roussillon and northern Spain. I had been particularly keen to mug up on the work of Gaudi. I noticed that Philippe Garner, in his book *Collecting Art Nouveau*, describes the architect's work as "uncompromisingly curvilinear".

When we saw Barcelona's Sagrada Familia in the flesh, "uncompromisingly curvilinear" seemed a very dry and inadequate description for an architecture in which stone forms seem to grow organically from the ground.

A batch of books which I purchased yesterday includes a *TV Fun Annual* from 1958.

I remembered that my parents had obtained their first television set in 1953 after winning second prize in a raffle - the set arrived just in time for the Coronation!

My favourite programme of the Fifties was *Mick and Montmorency*, starring the diminutive Charlie Drake and his much taller companion. The *Fun Annual* bills the pair as "The Long and the Short of It". Music Hall-style tag lines for TV acts were all the rage at the time. Examples from the 1958 annual are:

Charlie Chester - "Chin-up Boy"
Eddie Calvert - "Man with the Golden Trumpet"

Shirley Eaton - "The Modern Miss"
Diana Decker - "The Cutie Queen of the TV Screen"

I bought a presentation edition of an old *Guinness Book of Records* this afternoon.

The customer who sold me the book told me that this particular copy had been delivered to a customer by Brian Statham, the legendary Lancashire and England fast bowler. It seems that Statham became the Stockport representative for Guinness after his playing days were over.

Statham's international bowling partner, Freddie Truman, has honourable mention in the book. Statham's name does not appear.

Between the pages of Roger Wood's *Sadlers Wells Ballet* I found a wedding anniversary card inscribed "All our love and best wishes, Mum and Pops", and a programme for *La Sonnambula* at the Theatre Royal, Drury Lane.

These two objects conjured up a beautiful picture of a lovely evening.

I have just taken delivery of a 1950 edition of *The Saturday Book*, which contains a very odd article by John Arlott.

The piece, which is called *Round England with an Ear-trumpet*, lists pleasant and unpleasant English place-names. The pleasant ones include: Red Roses; Merry Maidens; Holme-next-the-Sea; Henley-in-Arden; Midsomer Norton. The unpleasant ones include: Peover Superior; Blubberhouses; Sour Milk Force; Ugley.

This brought to mind a piece of local history and also a piece of personal history:

The former inhabitants of the High Peak village of Bugsworth were so sensitive about their place-name that they had it changed to Buxworth.

I once went on a date with a girl called Sheila Sidebottom who insisted that her surname should be pronounced "Siddybottoom".

A collection of books which I bought today includes *Country Monuments* by Hugh Collinson. When I opened the book I found a typed fragment from a scientific paper:

"It is in this section that experience is most useful in indicating areas in which to search for an optimum since there are some quite strong interactions between some of the variable parameters and also the pricing of superconductors themselves is not an entirely logical process, yet it is a necessary consideration in order to determine the economic optimum".

Sounds like a candidate for Pseuds Corner in *Private Eye*!

A customer showed me an 1879 edition of Louisa M. Alcott's *Eight Cousins*. The book contains the following hand-written dedication:

"To the many boys and girls whose letters it has been impossible to answer, this book is dedicated as a peace offering by their friend. L. M. Alcott."

My customer asked me if the book was valuable. She was disappointed when I suggested that all the books in this edition probably contained identical copies of Ms Alcott's dedication to her readers.

However, I was intrigued by Ms Alcott's rather childish handwriting. One of my acquaintances once told me that she was able to read a person's character from their hand-writing. When I heard this I made a resolution that I would henceforth type all my letters to her!

I finally managed to obtain for Oliver a copy of *Wings of the Dawning - The Battle for the Indian Ocean*, by Arthur Banks. Oliver, who served in the Horn of Africa during the war, has a number of mentions in the book. Unfortunately, some allusions to his name in the index are accompanied by inaccurate page references.

I have a customer who works as an index-compiler. It struck me that she carries a very important responsibility.

Julian Barnes' *Letters from London* is worth buying for the index alone. Take the following entries:

Brown Ron MP: parliamentary record, 17; sexual record, 18; criminal record, 19-20.

Bruno Frank: almost hurts Mike Tyson 14; stars in Aladdin, 15.

World Cup: possible effect of England's 1990 defeat on Nicholas Ridley's politics, 50.

In one of my second-hand books I discovered a holiday postcard with the message:

"Just a line to let you know that we have arrived safely in Autria" (sic).

I looked across to the map section in the shop and noticed the French spelling on the Kunnerley & Frey map of Austria - "Autriche".

The regular *Guardian* cartoon strip *Lost Consonants* came to mind.

Andy and Hilary bought me Michael Palin's *Pole to Pole* for my birthday.

In the book there is a description of a meeting in Lindos between Michael and the astrologer Patric Walker. Patric told Michael that Astrology is an Art rather than a Science. This sounds to me like a clever alibi to explain away inaccurate predictions.

It is a pity that Michael Fish didn't make a similar statement about Meteorology before his failure to predict the London hurricane!

I sold a copy of Beverly Nichols' *Cry Havoc* this morning. When the book was first published in 1933, the *Manchester Guardian* said, "Here is a man who does actually feel a passionate hatred of war and the whole gang of warmongers - the devil's gambles of armaments manufacturers, the chauvinism of the commercial press, all the mean jumble of national spites and fears which are leading mankind up the next primrose path".

This afternoon I sold a copy of Crispin Aubrey and Paul Chilton's book, *1984 in 1984*. There is much in the book about Newspeak and the tyranny of language, and the authors demonstrate that the real 1984 was not so far removed from Orwell's vision as many people suppose.

I have vivid personal memories of the newspeak of 1984: unilateral disarmers like myself were branded by the press as "one-sided disarmers" and weapons of mass destruction were called "deterrents".

The attitudes which Beverly Nichols had described in 1933 were still with us in 1984.

According to my 1967 copy of *Collins Dictionary of First Names*, one of the abbreviated forms of Charlotte is 'Totty'.

I began to wonder about the wisdom of choosing Charlotte as a name for our daughter!

The local dentist showed me a letter which he had discovered between the leaves of a second-hand book. The letter was written by Sir Thomas Eric St. Johnston to Nancy Mitford. Sir Thomas informs Nancy that he has just written a book called *One Policeman's Lot*.

I am now carrying out a booksearch for a copy of *One Policeman's Lot*.

I noticed an article in the *Topical Times Football Book for 1962-63* about Liverpool football club, recent winners of the Second Division Championship, and their new manager Willie Shankly.

In subsequent years Liverpool would go on to much greater honours, and 'Willie' would become 'Bill'!

I found a remarkable confirmation of the Law of Averages in a *Playfair Cricket Annual*. The book contains a list of the number of occasions on which each country has won the toss in Test matches:

England	49.4%
Australia	47.7%
West Indies	52%
New Zealand	51%
India	50.2%
Pakistan	50%
Sri Lanka	50%
Zimbabwe	50%

In a copy of Haslett's *Unsolved Problems of Science*, I found a copy of the University of London examination paper in Mathematics from 1954. The examination rubric reads as follows:

"Full marks may be obtained for answers to about seven of the following ten questions"

My tidy, scientifically-trained mind tells me that this method of marking mathematics papers is mathematically unsound!

Books to suit all tastes.

Book Lovers

There are as many reasons for falling in love with a book as there are for falling in love with another human being.

Sometimes the attraction is purely physical - a nicely-bound volume, a well-illustrated text, a lurid dust-cover, a particular author's name on the cover. However, more discerning book-buyers look beyond surface impressions; some simply seek a good yarn, others cherish fine use of language, regardless of story-line. Some customers try to re-live the golden age of their childhood by seeking a copy of the book which caught their imagination long ago. Other people buy books to support a hobby.

Whatever their appeal, books make fine objects of desire: they will submit to endless readings, endure much caressing of their covers and turning of their pages - and they never answer back!

A book does not have to be in good condition for it to give pleasure. Terry comes into my shop on a regular basis to buy books on military topics. He is always careful to select books which are in a state of some dilapidation!

Terry is taking a book binding course and needs suitable material on which to practise.

One of my customers buys the novels of Helen McInnes - books which have given her much pleasure in her retirement. When I dropped off a McInnes novel at her house she showed me her book collection and also her autograph book, a superb collection of the signatures of actors and actresses from the golden age of theatre. Last month she ordered a copy of *Sisters in Arms*, the story of female gunners in the war. She told me that she had been just such a gunner in the last war. This week she ordered guidebooks to Orkney and Shetland - she is taking a holiday there later this year.

You find out so much about people from their books.

A man who is about to exchange life in a suburban semi for life on a houseboat offered to sell me his large personal library. He explained that there would be very little room for books in his floating home.

Is the loss of a lifetime's collection of books an acceptable price to pay for freedom?!

A customer bought a copy of Peter Mayle's *A Year in Provence*, to replace the copy which he had loaned to a friend and never had returned.

I told the customer how I had purchased my own copy of the book:

Having read pre-publication extracts from Mayle's book in one of the Sunday papers I decided that *A Year in Provence* would be ideal holiday reading on our vacation in Provence. On the way to France, we stopped off in London with the intention of buying a copy. Unfortunately, Mayle's book had sold out at every bookshop we tried. Finally, we came to Hatchard's in Piccadilly. Just as I was being given the familiar "Sorry, we have sold out" message at the counter, a customer returned a copy of the very book which I had been seeking so desperately.

Thanks to this unexpected opportunity I was able to read a chapter per day throughout our twelve-day stay in Avignon.

A customer asked me if I could supply her with play scripts which she could use to plan a "who-done-it?" weekend at her house. I offered to borrow some scripts from a friend in South Cave who is involved in amateur dramatics.

Tracy was kind enough to send me the following scripts: *A Touch of Danger*, by Francis Durbridge; *Murder in Company*, by Philip

King and John Boland; *Wanted - One Body*, by Raymond Dyer.

When the customer returned the plays to me a few weeks later, I wrote to Tracy as follows:

"I am returning the plays which you kindly sent me. The customer has used them to organise a 'Murder Weekend' at her home. I hope that you will not be cited as an accomplice when the trial comes up!"

This morning I held a conversation with a customer about the pleasure to be obtained from touching, stroking and even smelling a newly-acquired book. She told me of her shock when she had come across an advertisement for a piece of educational computer software which included the phrase "A better way to learn than reading a boring book". We agreed that a computer image could never replace the visual, tactile and even aromatic pleasure to be gained from a nicely-produced book.

I have one customer who uses books to stop smoking. If she did not have a novel in her hand she would be tempted to pick up a cigarette.

A customer came in today to buy Agatha Christie paperbacks.

She told me that they were for a German friend who is learning English by reading Miss Christie's crime novels.

A customer left me the following note with a request for books:

The Man Who Listens to Horses by Monty Roberts. Californian equine expert's memoirs, model for *The Horse Whisperer.*

The Island of the Day Before by Umberto Eco. Shipwreck near dateline is basis for more philosophical fireworks.

A customer asked if I would carry out a search for a book called *Living Without Cruelty*. She explained that she would like a copy of the book to loan to her friends.

"I am a passionate vegetarian, and I should like to convert my friends to the cause", she said. "But I do prefer this gentle form of propaganda, rather than verbal tub-thumping, don't you?"

This morning I took a telephone call from Norway. One of my customers has a Norwegian business client who is the proud owner of a vintage Alvis car. I was asked to search for a book on the history of the Alvis company. As I listened to the perfect English of the Norwegian businessman, I mused not only on the inability of the British to sustain an independent car industry, but also on our inability to speak foreign languages.

As one customer bought a book, he sighed and said, "That's my ration used up".

He explained to me that his wife would allow him to buy only one book per holiday.

A customer asked me to carry out a book-search for *To Elsie with Love*. She told me that Elsie was a Scottish spiritualist who held seances on three evenings per week. She was also my customer's grandmother.

One of my regular browsers was dragged out of the shop by his wife. As he was being pulled out of the door, he whispered:

"As you can see, I'm not a free agent this morning".

A customer came in today to buy reading matter for his month's tour of duty on a North Sea oil-rig. He bought six Flashman paperbacks.

A customer asked me to search for a book by Freya Stark.

Freya Stark's *Beyond Euphrates* was the first book which was made available to Terry Waite after thirteen months of solitary confinement.

Escapist reading!

Today, I sold a copy of the *Complete Works of Shakespeare*. I asked my customer if she was a Shakespeare enthusiast. "No", she said. "My husband wants the book as an aid for solving crossword clues".

One customer who bought a very nice, turn-of-the-century atlas from me this morning, told me that he would be in trouble when he returned home - he had been sent out by his wife simply to buy buns and sandwiches for lunch.

I wrapped up the atlas for him in a plain bag.

When he picked up the book, he dropped his sandwiches.

A large-format, illustrated learn-a-foreign-language book has been standing on my shelves for some weeks. This book invites the reader to learn a foreign language simply by memorising captions beneath pictures of everyday objects. I have tried in vain to identify the language on offer in this book. The text contains no clues as every caption is simply in the target language.

A customer who bought the book today finally put me out of my misery - he informed me that he is trying to acquire a smattering of Norwegian before embarking on a trip to the fjords.

A customer who is writing a history of the sidecar asked me to search for Henry Lowe Watson's *Adventures of a Dispatch Rider*.

Paul called for a book about antique coins. Yesterday he ran his metal detector over a Buxton field and discovered an Elizabethan coin.

Layers of human history are to be found below the surface of the Peak District much as geological time is recorded in rock strata.

The following quotation is pinned up in my shop:

"If a book is worth reading it is worth buying".
John Ruskin

The converse should also be true: "If a book is worth buying it is worth reading".

Rumour has it that some of the books at the top of the bestseller charts are bought merely as shelf decoration by many customers - presumably by the type of people who only purchase clothes which have designer labels.

How many people have bought *A Brief History of Time, Sophie's World, The Satanic Verses* or *A History of the World in 10 1/2 Chapters* have actually read them?

A customer asked me to direct him to the ufology section.

Just as I was about to confess my ignorance of this particular bibliographical category, he said:

"Do you have any books about unidentified flying objects?"

As soon as my customer had left the shop, I wrote out a new shelf sign and inaugurated High Street Bookshop's UFOLOGY section.

A lady customer bought her husband *The Observer Book of Aircraft* as a gift to thank him for shaving off his twenty year old goatee beard.

Shortly after the couple had left the shop, the husband called back in and told me in a conspiratorial whisper that he had only shaved off his beard so that he could grow a full set of moustache and beard without going through a period where his face would be a mosaic of stubble and full growth.

A customer came in for a copy of Charles Reade's *The Cloister and the Hearth*.

Reade's book made a deep impression on me when I first read it as a teenager. When I decided, in my twenties, that I would like to re-read the story, I had forgotten both the title of the book and the name of its author. My search for the book was to last for several months. I visited a large number of bookshops where I would flick through the pages of as many novels as possible, in the hope that ·I would recognise the story which had so caught my imagination. I well remember my joy when I finally located a copy in a bookshop in Commercial Street, Leeds.

My customer expressed her own admiration for *The Cloister and the Hearth*. She said that she could not understand why Reade's epic story had not been made into a film or a television serial. It seems that this is the ultimate accolade for any novel these days!

Many customers come into the shop to buy the book of a film which they have seen on television or in the cinema.

I have never been tempted to buy 'the book of a film', but I have often been disappointed when the characters in the film version of a book which I have read do not match the characters which I have conjured up in my imagination.

However, I have often bought a book which I have first heard as a reading on the radio. Examples:

Letters from my Father by Amanda Allsop
Life and Other Punctures by Eleanor Bron
Lake Wobegon Days by Garrison Keillor

This morning I sold a copy of the *McArthur Senate Hearings* from the Korean War period. The purchaser was a solicitor who is taking a master's degree. He is writing a thesis on "The Use of Biological Warfare".

A customer who is called Thelma asked me to search for a copy of Marie Correlli's *Thelma*. It seems that my customer's mother had chosen her daughter's name after reading Marie Correlli's book in the maternity ward.

A young man who purchased three books by Von Daniken told me that he was buying the books as preparation for a university course in Ancient History.

Is Von Daniken on his reading list?!

One customer comes in regularly to buy topographical books for his disabled, house-bound wife. He explains:

"My wife is able to travel the world through her books".

I obtained some Mary Englebreit books from the U.S.A. for a customer. They all have excruciatingly optimistic titles, such as *Don't Look Back, Home Sweet Home, Don't Waste the Miracle, A Good Marriage, Pals, She Who Loves a Garden*, but the illustrations are exquisite. My customer, who discovered Ms. Englebreit's work on a visit to the States, will be giving the books to friends for Christmas. She is keen for her friends to share in the pleasure which she obtained from these little works.

The pleasure of book-giving is being able to share one's own enjoyment of literature with others. This is also the joy of book-selling.

Last week a customer asked me to search for a book about the artist, George Richmond. She told me that one of her relatives would be appearing on Sunday's *Antiques Roadshow* with a painting by Richmond.

I watched the programme. The painting was valued at £60,000.

One customer made a purchase and then said to me: "You can be assured that the book is going to a good home. I think it's important to know that, don't you?"

I felt like a parent who has just offered a child for adoption.

Michelle told me about a bookseller she had encountered on a visit to Shropshire. He told Michelle that he was fond of taking a 'busman's holiday' to Hay-on-Wye, a town which contains more than twenty second-hand bookshops. The bookseller's wife, who was the only driver of the two, would drop him off at a bookshop with the parting words, "If you're not back here to meet me in an hour I shall drive off and leave you". On their last visit to Hay the bookseller had failed to meet his deadline and his wife had kept to her word. Divorce proceedings are now taking place.

Peak District Life

High Street Bookshop is a fine place from which to observe life in the Peak District. My daily journey to work takes me from my home town of Chapel-en-le-Frith across the Roman road which runs along the boundary between the Dark Peak and the White Peak; my early morning walk in Buxton takes me through the Pavilion Gardens, around the spa town and up the Slopes to the old market town: my shop window faces the town's Market Place; the Post Office, the newsagents, the dentist's surgery and the Methodist Church are all just across the road from my shop; and my customers bring me daily bulletins on the latest Buxton gossip.

A tourist who came into the shop this morning said he had never seen such a high concentration of public houses as there is on Buxton's High Street. I asked him if he was making a complaint.

"Yes", he said. "I've not brought enough money with me".

A man from Norfolk told me about his late wife. She was a great walker who loved the hills of the Peak District. Her ashes are scattered on Mam Tor.

When my customer is feeling low he makes the long drive from East Anglia to the Derbyshire hill. Once there, he sits in the car park and runs slowly through his memories.

One customer who came into the shop on this sunny, crisp autumn morning told me that she had just walked through the Pavilion Gardens where she had marvelled at the colours of the autumn trees. She said, "We do tend to take this beautiful town for granted. We should learn to stand and stare occasionally".

My son rang the shop this morning with a disturbing piece of information: a light aircraft had just crashed near Buxton.

A moment later, a fleet of fire engines and ambulances sped along High Street.

Five minutes later, Andy rang to tell me that an I.R.A. bomb had exploded in Manchester and injured 200 people.

The multi-million pound face-lift of Buxton's Crescent is almost complete and the long-awaited pedestrianisation and landscaping of Spring Gardens (the main shopping street) is also underway at last. Huge metal barriers have been placed around the many construction areas.

The drawing on this year's Christmas card from David Russell's Art Shop shows the partially-renovated Crescent viewed from behind the temporary railings at the end of Spring Gardens. Buxtonians will remember 1996 as 'The Year of the Barricades'.

A tourist on his first visit to town told me that he found Buxton "graceful and welcoming". When I asked him to elaborate he said, "The buildings are elegant and the people are friendly".

The Peak District is one of the busiest National Parks in the world - I discovered from a newspaper article today that only the Mount Fuji Park in Japan attracts more visitors.

Buxton stands outside the National Park boundary, but at the geographical heart of the Peak District. After reading the newspaper article, I thanked my lucky stars that my bookshop is located in such a honeypot. I then waited expectantly for the swarm of visitors!

When I took my early morning walk this morning, I noticed the usual queue of people waiting to fill their containers with Buxton spa water from St. Ann's Well.

The *Ward Lock Guide to Buxton* of 1908 quotes Dr Thresh's explanation for the miraculous properties of the waters:

"The presence of nitrogen and carbonic acid, in their nascent state, and the recent demonstration by Lord Rayleigh of the presence of argon and helium, and by Lord Blythswood of radium, may explain the action of these waters. The molecular activity of radium is the most powerful of any known body; and it is probable that, in combination with the above gases, it sets up a corresponding activity in the peripheral nerve endings of the tissues of the skin which is hence communicated throughout the whole system".

Given this simple explanation, I cannot understand why some people are so sceptical about the healing properties of the Buxton waters!

My window cleaner, who carries his ladders on the roof of a Reliant Robin, surprised me by coming in to buy a book about classic motorbikes. He told me that he is the proud owner of a Harley-Davidson. The bike is only used in fair weather, as it has large amounts of very rustable chromework. In summer, he houses the machine in his porch. In winter, he keeps the bike in his living room!

The reverse mirrors on his machine carry the legend, "Ride to Live. Live to Ride".

Having heard about his garaging arrangements, I couldn't help feeling that "Live with your Bike" would be a more appropriate motto!

The fair arrived on the Market Place today. As I look out of my shop window I can see that there is something for everyone: "white knuckle" rides for teenagers who enjoy being frightened to death; gentler rides for young children; dodgems for families; stalls for mums and dads.

Oliver told me of an occasion when the backcloth of the shooting gallery was punctured by a bullet which then went clean through the window of the Rates Office in the Town Hall.

I noticed that the shooting gallery had once again been placed in front of the Town Hall.

Shopkeepers in Higher Buxton have agreed that they will decorate their premises with hanging baskets during the summer months. The hanging basket on my shop hangs from the only available spot - just above head-height in the doorway of the shop.

Daily watering of the basket is essential, and the tiny blue plastic chair which I have in the Children's Corner is proving useful for this activity. I stand on the chair to carry out the watering of the basket and then hold the chair above my head as shelter from the dripping water when I walk back into the shop.

The Fair has arrived on the Market Place. Vivaldi's *Four Seasons* on the cassette recorder in my shop is competing with Elvis Presley's *Jailhouse Rock* which is booming out from the fairground ride across the road. The cacophony of sound is matched by the cacophony of people who are in town this week. Girls in tight jeans and bare midriffs and boys with well-worn jeans and tattooed arms are in Buxton for the fair; ladies in elegant black outfits and gentlemen in sandals and Panama hats are in town for the Opera Festival.

The funfair is in town and it is Festival-time at the Opera House. Cold, grey weather, which has hung over Buxton for days, has given way to clear blue skies. The grey old town has been transformed into a riot of colour, with decorative bunting everywhere.

I went for an early morning walk this morning and soaked in the atmosphere. When I walked down to the spa town I found that the forecourt of the Edwardian Opera House was being transformed into a pavement cafe. When I walked back up to the Market Place and looked at the fairground art on the closed stalls and rides of the funfair, I could almost hear the noise and bustle which will come to the Market Place when the fair opens later today.

One customer brought me a photo-copy of an old postcard of Buxton's High Street - the street on which my bookshop stands. The picture, which dates from about 1915, shows a fine French-like avenue of trees lining the northern side of the road. Unfortunately, all these trees were removed long ago when the road was widened to cope with increasing traffic.

Roads in Lower Buxton are currently being narrowed as part of a major traffic-calming and pedestrianisation scheme. In my home town of Chapel-en-le-Frith the main road, which was widened in 1936, has been narrowed back to its original proportions as part of traffic-calming measures.

If only traffic-calming measures had been fashionable eighty years ago, I would now have a view from my shop of a splendid line of trees!

A tourist on his first visit to Buxton looked out of my shop window at Higher Buxton's market place and said, "Is this the centre of town?"

When I told him about the existence of the spa town in Lower Buxton, he said, "Thank goodness. I was beginning to fear that this was all there is to the place".

So much for the attractions of Buxton's old market town!

A couple from Wolverhampton who came into the shop this morning told me that they have a static caravan in the Peak District village of Litton, which they try to visit at least once per month. Their idea of the perfect escape from the urban jungle of Wolverhampton is a walk with their dog along a Peakland trackway from Litton village to the George Inn at Tideswell.

They asked if I lived locally. I told them that I live in an old stone house in Chapel-en-le-Frith, that I have a panoramic view from my study window of the old Capital of the Peak, and that I am in the habit of taking a Sunday walk, with my family and my dog, along a Peakland trackway to Bowden Hall at the foot of South Head.

It struck me that my customer's monthly heaven is my everyday existence.

Robin Whiteman's book *The Yorkshire Moors and Dales* contains a photograph by Rob Talbot of the great gritstone ridge of Ellerkin Scar, which rises above Askrigg in the Yorkshire Dales. I was immediately struck by the uncanny resemblance between this picture and the view from my attic-study window of the high gritstone ridge of Combs Moss, which rises to the south of Chapel-en-le-Frith. The general contours of Combs Moss, the position of the trees on its slopes, the pattern of its field enclosures and the position of the settlement at its foot are all strikingly similar to the general contours and features of Ellerkin Scar.

A daily vision of the Yorkshire Dales in the heart of the High Peak is a welcome treat for a Yorkshireman now exiled in Derbyshire!

It is late January and Rev. Bob Davies at the Methodist Church is being kept very busy with funerals.

For the third time this week, I watched from the window of my bookshop as a large hearse and a posse of shiny black cars pulled up outside his church. One member of the funeral party was wearing a kilt together with full Scottish accessories. His tartan outfit seemed altogether too bright and gay for such a solemn occasion.

Then I remembered my brother-in-law's account of a funeral which he had attended last week. What began as a very sad occasion ended up as one of the best family get-togethers which he had attended in a long time!

I wondered if the kilted gentleman would end the day by dancing a Highland fling at the funeral party!

Before the shop opened this morning I walked down the Slopes to admire the newly-restored Crescent. Today's Guardian carries a picture of the renovated building with the caption, "Once the most notorious Grade 1 listed building at risk in England."

The Crescent, "once the most notorious Grade 1 listed building at risk in England."

I am collecting material for a *Higher Buxton Town Trail*, which I am putting together for Higher Buxton Traders Association.

After closing the shop today I walked down to Dale Road to look at Buxton's little known, but splendid Arts and Crafts church. As is so often the case these days, the door to the church was locked. I was lucky enough to spot a churchwarden who was on his way to the building, and he was kind enough to let me in. I remembered Sylvia Plath's experience when she arrived at the locked Matisse chapel at Vence, in the South of France:

"I stared with my face through the barred gate. I began to cry. I knew it was so lovely inside, pure white with the sun through blue, yellow and green stained windows.

Then I heard a voice, "Ne pleurez, cntrez", and the Mother Superior let me in, after denying all the wealthy people in cars.

I just knelt in the heat of the sun and the colours of sky, sea, sun, in the pure white heart of the chapel. "Vous êtes si gentille", I stammered. The nun smiled. "C'est la miséricorde de Dieu". It was."

Dr Hall, author of *Georgian Buxton*, came into the shop today. He bought a number of books to support the research he is doing for his forthcoming work on John Carr, the architect of Buxton's famous Crescent.

Conversation turned to the Crescent, which is now being fully restored after years of shameful neglect. I suggested to Dr Hall that the design of the building owes very little, other than its overall shape, to the crescents of Bath. The architectural detailing on the Buxton building is very different from the styling on the Bath crescents and, to my mind, is much superior. Dr Hall said that he was glad to hear my comment. He regards Carr as a true original and an architect well ahead of his time.

We both worried about the future of Buxton's Crescent. Flats for retired people are planned for some of the floors in the restored building. But Dr Hall has some doubts about the suitability of high-ceilinged Georgian rooms as homes for retirees.

Higher Buxton is a collection of old stone houses and inns set about a large market place. The fabric and traditional character of the Old Town are largely intact, but the view of Market Place from the window of my bookshop does include two late twentieth century additions - a night club and a supermarket.

The supermarket is of very modest dimensions. Two much larger supermarkets are located on the perimeter of Lower Buxton.

Jo-Ann and I know a supermarket in the South of France which is so vast that the shelf-stackers go about their business on roller skates!

A customer told me about a research project which she is carrying out into the Peak District custom of well-dressing. When she discovered that I am Chairman of Chapel-en-le-Frith Well-dressing Committee, she asked for an interview:

Q.   Has well-dressing become commercialised?

A.   Yes. But towns which dress their wells are not just bringing in the tourists; they are keeping alive a wonderful local custom.

Q.   What makes a successful well-dressing?

A.   Strict adherence to traditional rules about the exclusive use of natural materials, combined with a novel approach. In Chapel we use a unique quadripartite board and we design our picture-panels on computer - We advertise ourselves as the Peak District's only hi-tech well-dressing!

Q.   What function does well-dressing have in the community?

A.   For the dressers, it is a joint venture which allows individuals to express their talents - artistic, practical and organisational. For all the townspeople, it is an expression of pride in their town.

Chapel's first well-dressing after the revival of the custom.

Jo-Ann took my place in the shop for half-an-hour on this beautiful sunny day. I purchased a bag of chips and walked over to the Slopes to eat them and to enjoy the view and the fresh air.

These steep gardens were formerly used for exercise by patients who had taken the Buxton Water Cure. Those who reached the summit could enjoy a superb bird's-eye view of the spa town and its surrounding hills. Today, foliage obscures the view, but the prospect is no less satisfying. The visitor who is prepared to dodge about between the trees experiences a series of visual surprises as individual buildings come into view, one-by-one.

What a Picture!
What a Photograph!

My most used visual aid for Current Affairs lessons with the Sixth Form was an old copy of John Terraine's *The Mighty Continent*. The book has a lengthy and informative text, but more importantly it contains a superb selection of photographs which give a disturbing visual record of life in the Twentieth Century - wounded soldiers from the Boer War laid out on the floor of a squalid room; Congolese boys whose hands have been cut off in a punishment inflicted by their Belgian rulers; troops and demonstrators in confrontation in front of the Winter Palace in St. Petersburg on Bloody Sunday, 1905; a burning fighter aircraft falling from the sky in the Great War; bodies in the trenches of the Somme; an aerial view of the devastation of Ypres in 1918; Lenin in Red Square in 1919; a family of starving Russian peasants in the famine which killed two million people; Hitler posing by the Landsberg City Gate after his release from prison in 1924; the dejected figure of an unemployed man on the streets of Wigan in the

1930s; Hitler marching through a sea of salutes at a Nuremberg Rally in 1934; angry protesters shaking their fists at German troops entering Prague in 1939; a German family who have been bombed out of their house in 1945; child victims at Belsen; a soldier raising the Soviet flag on the roof of the Reichstag above a devastated Berlin; a shaven-headed collaborator, baby in her arms, being taunted through the streets of a French town; the barricades of Paris in 1968; demonstrators shaking their fists at Russian soldiers entering Prague in 1968 (a re-run of the 1939 photograph); a small boy throwing stones at the troops in Belfast.

A single telling photograph can sometimes do the work of hundreds of descriptive words.

Edna O'Brien's book *Mother Ireland* contains a photograph of a group of nuns at Seapoint, County Dublin. Edna has given the picture a wonderful caption:

People say to one another "Do you think that nuns still wear the long stockinet navy-blue knickers, or have they kept up with the times and wear panties that match their new habits?"

I took delivery of several volumes in the *Sunday Times World Library Series*.

The volume which is devoted to France contains a photograph of a square in the Provencal town of Vence. A scruffily-clad artist, who has spent the morning hard at work on ceramics, is washing the clay from his hands at the fountain. One young woman is watching the scrubbing operation with some fascination, but she shows no interest in the artist himself. Everyone else simply walks by without giving the man a second glance.

The artist in the picture is none other than Marc Chagall!

An edition of *The Wonder Book of the Farm*, which was published shortly after the Second World War, contains a photograph of a battery system with the following caption: "Each hen has her own feed and water troughs, and when she lays an egg it rolls out of her reach, for birds kept in these conditions have a tendency to egg-eating".

In the text there is some acknowledgement of public concerns about the new system. But within a few years farms would be housing as many as four hens per cage - a cage with a width less than the wing span of just one bird!

I bought a copy of Denis Healey's book of photographs, *Healey's Eye*.

Denis' book includes a page from a photograph album of a school camp. One photograph, captioned *The Shirtless*, shows a group of boys by a river. One of the boys is bending over and exposing a pair of bare buttocks to Denis' camera. Denis Healey as a budding Robert Mapplethorpe!

I acquired a copy of Lesley Bailey's *B.B.C. Scrapbook Vol 1 (1896-1914)*. The book contains a wonderful photograph from 1907. The picture shows four immaculately-clad ladies playing diabolo on a road-side verge whilst their men-folk struggle to repair a broken-down car. This image is a neat reversal of a mental picture of gender roles in *Sport* and *Labour* which I have carried in my mind ever since I heard the following announcement at a football match at Elland Road:

"Message for Mr Brown in the South Stand. Your wife has just given birth to a baby boy".

Theatre in the Hills, Ros McCoola's book about Buxton's Opera House, contains a marvellous photograph of a group of 'luvvies' from the Buxton Repertory Company of 1948.

A score of actors and actresses are featured in the photograph, but it is the wonderfully-flirtatious behaviour of Jacqueline Barnett which catches the eye. Jacqueline, a Lucille Ball look-a-like, has her left arm firmly linked through Denis Banyard's arm and her right arm linked through Liam Gaffney's arm, but she is cheekily bending over to sup from a cup of tea which is being held by the suave, handsome Liam.

I showed the photograph to Oliver, who pointed out that the picture also features Gwen Watford, Mary Sanderson and Shaun Sutton, all of whom went on to higher things. I wonder if their later theatrical experiences were quite so enjoyable as their days with Buxton rep!

A customer who bought a book on Cezanne told me she had just returned from a visit to the Cezanne exhibition in London. She offered to loan me the exhibition catalogue.

On one page of the catalogue there are two contrasting paintings of Mont Sainte-Victoire, one by Cezanne, one by Renoir. Cezanne's picture of the mountain is highly geometric, almost cubist. Renoir's portrait is much more about light than about solid forms. But these two contrasting pictures reflect with equal accuracy my own memories of the mountain.

A couple of years ago we made an overnight stop in our touring caravan at a service station near Mont Sainte-Victoire. When we emerged from the van in the early hours of the morning, we saw the very image which Cezanne had depicted. Every crease, fold and shadow on the mountain was highlighted in the morning light. We were looking at a landscape which seemed to be made out of crêpe paper. On another occasion, we drove past the mountain at mid-day and saw the very scene which Renoir had depicted. The light was strong and all solid forms had dissolved. The road was dappled with shadow and sunlight, and the mountain was a background of shimmering haze.

I have acquired a copy of Trevor Francis' *World Cup Football Annual for 1983*.

The cover of the book features a photograph of Trevor taken at a floodlit game. A light from somewhere in the main stand appears on the photograph as a circular white glow just above the player's head. On first glance, the white sphere looks like a tennis ball which Trevor is about to head. A more generous interpretation would be that Trevor is wearing a halo!

I should not make fun of Trevor. His son, Matthew, is an ex-pupil of mine. When I retired from the headship of Silverdale School, Trevor kindly presented me with a bottle of pink champagne.

As I shelve the paperbacks which come into the shop, I am all too aware of the importance which publishers attach to the design of book-covers. Once-upon-a-time, book covers were splendidly plain. On the original Penguin paperbacks, the mere presence of a small penguin motif on orange and white card was all that was required to signal the literary quality between the covers. In recent years, covers have become more and more graphic and lurid. But there are some interesting exceptions:

Nicholson Baker's highly explicit novels, *Vox* and *The Fermata*, both have very plain jackets. When I pick up these books I feel as if I am receiving pornography through the post in plain-wrappers.

The cover for the paperback version of Martin Amis' much-hyped novel *The Information* is entirely plain except for the single motif of a lower-case *'i'*. This strikes me as a rather odd marketing ploy

- why advertise a story about jealousy as if it were a leaflet from a tourist information centre?

The Power of Poetry

Dylan Thomas gave the following definition of poetry:

"Poetry is what makes me laugh or cry or yawn, what makes me want to do this or that or nothing".

In an old edition of *The Real McGonagall - Poetic Gems from the Works of the Poet and Tragedian, William McGonagall*, I found a cutting from the Sunday Times. In the newspaper article, the Rt. Hon. Thomas Johnston explains that McGonagall always had problems when composing the last line of a stanza. He quotes, by way of illustration, McGonagall's Jubilee Ode:

"For sixty glorious, magnificent years has reigned our noble Queen,
And her reign has been the most beautiful that has ever been seen,
Since she went up the throne the world has grown,
For instance, we've seen the rise and progress of the bicycle, the telegraph and the telephone."

I discovered another wonderful example in *The Real McGonagall*:

"Beautiful Railway Bridge of Tay,
Alas! I am very sorry to say,
That ninety lives have been taken away,
On the last Sabbath Day of 1879,
Which will be remembered for a very long time."

Spike Milligan often has audiences in stitches with his wonderful readings of McGonagall's poems. However, McGonagall's own public readings were received with rather less enthusiasm. When he was pelted by an egg during one performance, McGonagall responded in his own inimitable poetic style. He shouted to his assailant:

"No egg
I beg."

Jackie, a former nurse, is one of my regular customers.

One day a patient died whilst in Jackie's care, and she was held responsible. Haunted by the memory of that day, Jackie seeks therapy through poetry. She has written hundreds of poems. Most of her poems are about her continuing life set against the death of her patient; some are about her search for love. Jackie gave me a booklet containing 70 of her poems. Poem No. 10 reads:

"I think of the man who died in my arms,
My body awakes to the sound of alarms.
Here I am in this lonely existence,
My mind constantly in rewind persistence.

Why did I lose you? See you slip away,
on the 25th March, a very sad day.
What are you doing? Can you see me?
What have I done? Can you hear me?
Please forgive me for what happened to you -
I had to stay on the Earth, in this life,
Where I live in turmoil and everyday strife.
Wherever you are - the life you're travelling,
I'm on it too - except I'm struggling.
One day I hope that we will meet,
So I can apologise at your feet."   *© Jackie Redhead*

Poem No. 57 reads:

"While some are laughing,
Some are crying.
While some are living,
Some are dying.

While some are winning,
Some are losing.
While some are gaining,
Some are failing.

While some are giving,
Some are taking.
While some are loving,
Some are hating.

While some are eating,
Some are starving.
While some are beginning,
Some are ending."   *© Jackie Redhead*

Michelle loaned me Halliday and Umpleby's *White Rose Garland*, a wonderful collection of Yorkshire dialect poems. My favourite poem in the book is *Aar Maggie*, which begins with the lines:

"Aw believe aar Maggie's courtin'
Fur shoo dresses hersen sa smart,
An' shoo's allus runnin ta t'winda,
When ther's any o' t'chaps abaat."

News is just out that Britain's favourite post-war poem is *Warning* by Jenny Joseph. The poem opens with the line:

"When I am an old woman I shall wear purple."

I seem to have reached an age where I can appreciate these sentiments.

The *Reader's Digest Book of the Human Body (1961)* contains a chapter by Dr John Hall entitled *Your Mind Can Keep You Well*. Dr Hall advises: "Learn to like people and resolve "I'm going to keep my attitude and thinking as pleasant and cheerful as possible"."

My mother was living proof of the soundness of this advice. She was always positive, always optimistic, and always thought the best of everyone she met. She cared a great deal for others who were ill or in distress, but she very rarely saw a doctor herself. Her philosophy of life was based on a poem which she had learnt at school. My mother died last week, aged 91. I read the poem at her funeral:

"Always make the most of life,
Lose no happy days.
Time will never bring thee back,
Chances swept away."

"Grumbling, grousing, discontent, cross, impatient with your lot,
Brings you something that's not wanted.
Something worse than you have got.
Be content - let this impress you,
Lives are mostly what we make them."

Acknowledgements

Text Credits

Text extracts from the following sources are reprinted with kind permission of the publishers and copyright holders stated. We apologise to those people whom we have been unable to trace for permission before going to print. Should any copyright holder have been inadvertently omitted they should apply to the publishers who will be pleased to acknowledge them in full in any subsequent editions.

Page 9   Article with kind permission of Ronald Proctor
Page 19   Terry Lamsley, *Conference with the Dead* (Ashtree Press)
Page 20   Letter with kind permission of Chris Bonington
Page 28   Joyce Critchlow, *Recipies from a Rectory Kitchen* (Marshall Pickering)
Page 32   Alan Bennett, *Writing Home* (Faber & Faber)
Page 32   Alan Sillitoe, *Life Without Armour* (Flamingo)
Page 37   *Buxton Guidebooks* (High Peak Borough Council)
Page 41   Extracts from *Wisdens Cricketers' Almanack* by kind permission of John Wisden & Co Ltd
Page 76   *Shell Guide to England* (Michael Joseph for Shell-Mex & BP)
Page 78   *Following the Fairways* (Kensington West)
Page 81   R McKenney & R Bransten, *Here's England* (Rupert Hart-Davis)
Page 83   Ashley Courtney, *Let's Halt Awhile in Great Britain* (Barrie & Monckliff)
Page 84   Humphrey Pakington, *English Villages and Hamlets* (B T Batsford)
Page 87   Extract from letter with kind permission of Tony Francis and Charley Eckhardt
Page 95   Jill Dick, *Writing for Magazines* (A & C Black)
Page 148   Julian Barnes, *Letters from London*
Page 177   Sylvia Plath, *Letters Home* (Faber & Faber)
Page 182   Edna O'Brien, *Mother Ireland* (Weidenfield & Nicholson)
Page 190   Poems reprinted with kind permission of Jackie Redhead

Picture Credits

Photographs and drawings by the author, other than:

Cover   (Shop interior) Jo-Ann Smith
Page ix   Photograph outside shop, Jo-Ann Smith
Page 77   Photograph of Buxton, with kind permission of High Peak Borough Council
Page 89   Photograph of author, Bob Bonsall

Other Credits

The author would like to thank all staff at ALD Design & Print for the care which they have taken during the preparation of this book and also Oliver Gomersal for his help with proof reading.

About the Author

Mike Smith was born in Leeds in 1942. He is a graduate of the University of Leeds where he read Chemistry. Mike has spent thirty years as a secondary school teacher. From 1987 to 1995 he was headteacher of Silverdale School, Sheffield, a comprehensive school with a high academic reputation.

Mike retired from full-time teaching in 1995 in order to devote time to selling and writing books and to local politics. He lives in Chapel-en-le-Frith where he is working hard, as a Parish Councillor and member of Chapel Amenity Society, on Operation Facelift, a plan to regenerate the old Capital of the Peak. He is also Chairman of the local Well-Dressing Committee. Mike is the author of a number of publications about Peak District towns and villages, including *The Look Again Guide to the Peak* (Caron Publications, 1989) and *Chapel-en-le-Frith in Old Picture Postcards* (European Library Publications, 1995). He has written articles for a variety of publications, including *The New Scientist*, *Modern Painters* and *The Dalesman*.

Mike runs High Street Bookshop, a second-hand bookshop in the Peak District spa town of Buxton.

About the Publisher

ALD Design & Print, established in 1988, has grown from humble beginnings in a spare bedroom at home to the company as it is today. With a fully self contained production system from design to final print using modern computerised systems.

Alistair Lofthouse, who is himself a former student of Mike Smith at Silverdale School in Sheffield, graduated from Sheffield Polytechnic with a degree in Design in 1988. In partnership with Elizabeth Mottram, a qualified teacher and, aided by their Production Manager and Editor Andrew Billingham, also a former student of Silverdale School, Alistair decided to try his hand at publishing with ALD's first book *Mi-Amigo, The Story of Sheffield's Flying Fortress*. This book tells the story of an American Flying Fortress and its brave crew which tragically crashed in Endcliffe Park, Sheffield in 1944. Written by David Harvey the book has sold successfully since it was released early 1997.

Alistair, with a great interest in local military history, is presently writing a book himself entitled *The Shiny Sheff - the Story of Sheffield's Fighting Ships*, which he is hoping to publish for release towards the end of 1997 to complement *Mi-Amigo*.